HERDING
BEANS

Short Stories From My Walk With God

LINDA PENTON

WESTBOW
PRESS
A DIVISION OF THOMAS NELSON

WestBow Press books may be ordered through booksellers or by contacting:

WestBow Press
A Division of Thomas Nelson
1663 Liberty Drive
Bloomington, IN 47403
www.westbowpress.com
1-(866) 928-1240

Because of the dynamic nature of the Internet, any web addresses or links contained in this book may have changed since publication and may no longer be valid. The views expressed in this work are solely those of the author and do not necessarily reflect the views of the publisher, and the publisher hereby disclaims any responsibility for them.

Any people depicted in stock imagery provided by Thinkstock are models, and such images are being used for illustrative purposes only.

Certain stock imagery © Thinkstock.

ISBN: 978-1-4497-5815-8 (hc)
ISBN: 978-1-4497-5813-4 (sc)
ISBN: 978-1-4497-5814-1 (e)

Library of Congress Control Number: 2012911628

Printed in the United States of America

WestBow Press rev. date: 10/02/2012

Table of Contents

To the Glory of God

As for me and my household,
we will serve the Lord!
Joshua 24:15

For my grandchildren
Signe and Sven

Acknowledgments

For many years, people have encouraged me to write the stories I tell and have them published. That has been a much bigger task than I thought it would be, partially because I am still involved in running a household and business, but also because I needed to reach into memories I have long since shut up, bring them out, dust them off and reexamine them. This has been a fun experience and at times heartrending as I remembered people and events long past. This book would not have come to fruition without the influence and encouragement of more than a few people to whom I wish to express my gratitude:

The publisher WestBow Press who walked me through the process of publishing this book so patiently.

My grandparents and parents who, throughout their lives modeled Christian faith and instilled in me a good work ethic and how to persevere in times of adversity.

Those teachers who enabled me to read and write the English language fluently and who encouraged me to express myself. These people gave selflessly and probably never realized how much their instruction was appreciated: My first-grade teacher, Mrs. Opsal, who kindly took my hand and helped me trace my first letters; Mary Schuster, who inspired a love for reading good stories in grades five and six; Mr. Jeal, the proper British gentleman, who brought into each class an appreciation for the Queen's English by insisting on proper pronunciation and punctuation in the seventh grade; Mr. Ast, who taught me as

I entered high school how to focus in order to achieve the highest standards in whatever I attempt; Mr Kahanoff, who taught English literature and journalism, without whose care and encouragement I would have been lost in the confusion of the big city school with no hope or direction. W. O. Mitchell, who became my friend and inspired me to write my own stories. Your advice as my mentor at the seminar at The Banff School of Fine Arts was invaluable. You continue to "free fall" in the universe of writers whom you inspired!

I also wish to recognize those spiritual leaders, teachers, and pastors without whose guidance, teaching, and prayers I would have been lost: My first Sunday school teacher, Agnes, whose teaching laid a foundation for understanding who God is; Rev. and Mrs. Unrau for offering me shelter in the great blizzard of 1961 and for their guidance to me as a teenager; Rev. Ron Kernahan and Mary. Without you I would have given up. You embody the love that Christ taught us.

Erny and Selma Radke, dear friends in Christ, who have loved me through the good times and the bad; Rev. Pat Langois, my friend and spiritual support when I moved to the foothills of Alberta and began an intense time of Bible study and self-examination.

My friends, past and present, who have provided the springboard from which my life takes direction. Without your friendship, my life would be so empty.

Richard who has provided technical support and computer training.

The artist Mark Rohl, who has interpreted the essence of each story so succinctly.

But most especially I want to thank my family:

Timothy Axel, Jill, and my two grandchildren, Signe and Sven, as well as my daughter, Bobbi Lynn, who encouraged me to write and then listened endlessly to the rewrites and Peter who has helped me understand how to use the computer program. You have laughed with me, shed tears with me, and offered constructive criticism. Thank you for making a mother proud.

My daughter-in law, Jill, for giving time she really didn't have to edit and correct my writing flubs. I thank you! You are a sweetheart!

My brother Ernest who has been a surrogate father to me. Thank you for teaching me to skate, swim, and play baseball. Thank you for teaching me the social graces so that I did not turn out to be a little barbarian! You offered encouragement and provided a sounding board for my ideas. So often you were the memory bank for details, dates, and funny incidents from my childhood that are part of this book. Thank you for giving me your love and support through the years!

My sister, Mildred, who taught me to be artistic and express my feelings at an early age. Thank you for helping me overcome my fears when I began school and later when I needed to be strong as a single mother.

My sister, Ethel and her husband, Mel who took in a headstrong teenager in grade eleven and helped to guide me through those rough waters until I became an independent young woman. I'm so fortunate to have you as my family.

And I thank you, the reader, for taking the time to read my stories. Although this book is filled with stories that are based on true incidents, I admit they have been enhanced by imagination where passing time and fading memory have erased details. If while reading you remember things differently, I beg your forgiveness. I hope you find enjoyment, humour, and inspiration from what I have written.

PART I

Be happy, young man, while you are young,
and let your heart give you joy in the
days of your youth.

Eccleciastes11:9a

Remember your Creator in the
days of your youth,
Before the days of trouble come.

Ecclesiastes12:1

Prologue I

Memories

I began writing these stories about ten years ago at the urging of my children and friends. I think they thought that if I was engaged in writing, I would be less inclined to bend their ears with the telling. Little did they know!

Storytelling has become an integral part of my life and is as natural to me as breathing. The tradition of sharing stories evolved from the bedtime stories my parents, especially my father, told us about the "olden days." I was born when my father was fifty, the last child in a family of five, and thought of my parents' younger years as ancient history. My siblings had left home by the time I was seven, so I grew up as if I were an only child and remember sitting with my father in the rocking chair, listening to stories about his life or those he was talented enough to invent in order to entertain me.

Growing up for me was like waking from a deep sleep, slowly becoming cognizant of my surroundings and how the world functioned around me. I was incredibly curious and filled with wonder, but most of all, I was in awe of the presence of God in the universe. By the time I was ten, I was often overwhelmed and filled with excitement that the Creator of all this would take notice of me!

Although we attended the little Baptist church fairly regularly, weather and roads permitting, Mom and Dad never forced 'religion' upon us but left us to explore the facets of our own relationship with God and discover what that might entail for us. For this I am eternally grateful!

I was always a serious child, thinking deeply about philosophy and religion, and loved engaging others in discussions about these matters. Although I have travelled extensively and broadened my horizons, growing up on the farm gave me a very earthy foundation, which has never failed to ground me in times of distress.

Let me invite you on a journey from 1911 to the present. I hope these very personal stories from my life will bring you laughter and inspiration. By sharing them, I hope to both entertain and give you pause to think. Enjoy!

Herding Beans

I came to work looking tired and a little disheveled on that Friday in November. When my coworkers inquired why I was not my usual self, I explained that I had been up late herding beans.

"Herding beans! Whatever do you mean?"

So here is the story.

Since I left my father's farm in Saskatchewan at age sixteen, I have not had aspirations to herd any kind of animal! Spending those first sixteen years of life with animals and herding them either convinces one that that is a great way of life or that it is not. Trying to bring the milk cows home from the grazing pasture and other herding adventures with chickens and ducks did not fulfill my teenage expectations and convinced me that it was *not* a great way of life!

Back then, the dog, Collie, usually helped with fetching the cows, but he also liked to go off with Dad to the field where he could lie in the shade of the truck all day, share Dad's lunch, and chase the odd rabbit that Dad would scare out of the stubble—if he had enough energy and the spirit so moved him. Anyway, the spirit did not move Collie to help me get those capricious cows home very often, so I was forced to run after them by myself.

There was one cow in particular who, upon seeing me coming over the hill, would put up her tail and literally head for the hills at the opposite end of the pasture. Then I would be obliged to play the game of roundup until I was worn out and practically in tears with frustration. By the time I managed to convince her to get on home to the barn for milking, I was calling her some pretty nasty names.

She was really a very lazy cow but because she did not like to be milked or disturbed she would come out of her lethargic state in a frenzy of bucking and kicking only to torment the humans who were attempting to care for her. I remember well my older brother, Ernie preparing to milk her. He would come with two sets of hobbles, which he applied to both front and back feet. Next, he would use a long piece of rope to bind her bodily to the pole fence with several wraps. Then he would apply a well-placed boot to her ribs, making her deflate a little in order to pull the rope tighter like a cinch so she couldn't wiggle out of it while milking was still in progress. Next, he would snub her head so close to the rail that she could hardly blink. Even then she would twitch and shudder as if he were torturing her and try to bat him with her stub of a tail, the only appendage still left unfettered. Therefore, Ernie's last heroic measure was to capture her tail so that it could be tied to her leg tightly with a good length of binder twine. That tail was not so much used to chase flies from her back as it was to club the side of his head when he sat down to milk her. She had acquired that club-like tail as a result of her favourite pastime, which was lying down to chew her cud and sleep on a pile of straw. On that fateful winter evening, she lay down for a long nap as usual. Her tail, however, was dangling into a puddle of water, where it was frozen fast by morning. Upon waking, she rose and heaved herself free of its icy grasp but left a good length of the tassel and a broken, bleeding piece of her tail in the ice. The tail healed. Her personality, however, did not!

Anyway, if you didn't snug that tail down quite right, she would somehow wiggle it free by the time you were halfway through milking and lambaste the side of your head with it. On one such occasion, my brother could see her tail coming loose, so, unwilling to suffer another blow from it, he set the milk pail aside, leaving it near the cow while he went into the barn to find a longer piece of twine. Upon his return, he found our very spoiled, two-year-old sheep buck, Lambkin, who had been pail fed, shoulder deep in the milk pail having breakfast. I don't know if my brother was angrier at the cow, the sheep, or himself for the loss of his hard-won prize of a half pail of milk.

Was it any wonder that this innocent-looking, white-and-brown bovine with the big, liquid eyes earned the name Nincompoop? We called her Ninny for short. In our dictionary, the definition for the word *frustration* was comprised of just one word: ninny!

I really don't understand why Dad kept her, except that she did produce a beautiful, healthy calf every spring, which he promptly removed from her care and influence. To his credit, he had once tried to take her to town to "ship her," which meant she would be sold to a packing plant for hamburger because she was old and of no distinguishable breed. On that occasion, he had spent most of the morning trying to get her loaded into the truck and, after succeeding, went into the house to clean up for the trip to town. Upon his return, he found her hanging half in and half out of the truck box, and the wooden stock rack, which measured a good six feet high, was broken beyond repair. So he gave that up as a bad cause, fearing that she would hurt herself or cause him to have an accident while driving. Dad unloaded her and released her back to a life of bovine pursuits: sleeping, chewing her cud, and tormenting the humans who cared for her. Ninny continued to be the bane of our existence until she died of old age while lying quietly and chewing her cud under the poplar trees.

Now considering my experiences with Ninny, you may understand why I removed myself from the confines of the family farm to attend school in the big city, where I married, had children, and developed a business career.

Later in life, I found that the selective memory of passing time had sifted through all the events of my years growing up on the farm and kept only a few pleasant and poignant, if somewhat unrealistic, memories that evoked a longing to have cows in my life once more. The trials and frustrations of herding, milking, and caring for those cows had faded into the dull recesses of memory past. Only some of the more pleasant memories of living in the country remained. Therefore, at the age of fifty-two, I was leaping at the chance to buy a small acreage where I could build a country home.

My husband and I had talked of retiring to a country home during our years of working in the city and speculated on the ins-and-outs and ups-and-downs of owning a small acreage, but that's as far as it went. When my husband passed away quite suddenly in 1998, not only was I left alone and bereft at the age of forty-nine, but I also found that all the plans we had made to sell our dry-cleaning business and travel had taken a sharp turn to the left and disappeared. I had no desire to travel alone and had to take a long, hard look at my economic situation. In the first place, I was too young to retire and needed to keep the business for mental health and financial reasons. During the first two or three years after he had passed, my son came to work with me at our dry cleaners and we threw ourselves into expanding the business and I joined a ladies service club. This I found was a lot of busywork with very little by way of spiritual reward.

Then one Sunday that was to become a decisive turning point in my life, I went for a drive back to the area in the foothills where my husband and I had often gone to have picnics on Sunday afternoons. The foothills of Alberta are not so different from the Cypress Hills of Saskatchewan, and I had always felt the pull of the gently rolling hills with hay bales and cows in the fields. On this particular drive, the old dream to retire to the country came back stronger than ever. Why couldn't I move to the country on my own? After all, this was the year 2000, and women in Canada had been experiencing liberated and entrepreneurial lives since sometime in the 1960s. The wheels were in motion—at least, the wheels that generated ideas.

Now my dear, departed mother, if you could have met her, would have warned you about my ability to dream up schemes and manufacture ideas. One of her favourite statements was, "Linda gets ideas that a cat wouldn't eat!" However, Mom's opinion notwithstanding, the idea to buy a country home became firmly entrenched. After another month or so of reading real estate ads and watching rising prices, I was thoroughly convinced this was the right move for me, and so I was bitten by the real estate bug. Then one day, I found The Ad, which read, "Acreage in the beautiful community of Millarville, drilled well and electricity on property. Small studio ideal for artist. Assumable mortgage at 6.5 percent." I knew this was my chance!

I went! I looked! I fell in love! It had a view of the valley and Rocky Mountains as well as a lovely stand of natural forest. The studio was really a garage package that the former owners had built and finished inside. Although it needed work, as no one had used it in a while, the possibilities were there.

One year later, my house in Calgary had been sold, and the cabin, as we now called it, had been renovated. All my worldly goods were packed into that tiny cabin, leaving only enough room to navigate between the stacks of boxes. It took another year to draw the plans and build my dream house near the front of the lot, where I had a spectacular view of the valley with a small swatch of the Rocky Mountains in the distance. Little did I know that that year would stand out as one of the most relaxing and creative years of my life. I learned so many new things, met new friends, and was inspired by the scenery of the foothills and new friendships to begin writing short stories and poetry. Here I have found healing from my grief, peace, and inspiration.

My children and I named the property Aspen Croft in tribute to my late husband's British heritage. A croft is a small parcel of land, so the name seemed appropriate, as the acreage measured approximately four acres. Within a year of moving, my son Axel and his wife, Jill, joined me, and we continue to enjoy life in this community with their two beautiful babies. These days, if you come to visit, you can literally hear that old song "Home Home on the Range" playing in my living room. My grandchildren love the children's movie *Home on the Range*, in which the cow, Grace, sings that song badly out of tune.

So it was not surprising to find ourselves discussing the pros and cons of having an animal or two on the property with some relatives who thought it would be great to have fresh milk and to make butter and cheese as we used to back on the farm in Saskatchewan. I, however, knew that the idea must remain on hold. Our business kept my son and I way too busy in Calgary for even the dream of taking on the added responsibility of cows at the moment.

That conversation about cows came back to haunt me one evening, though, when at eleven p.m., I was forced to herd beans in my kitchen. You're thinking, "Herd Beans!? This is how this story started, and we still don't know what this woman is talking about!"

Patience! Now that I've laid the groundwork, I will explain. Every year since we moved to the acreage, we host an open house for family, friends, and neighbors on the second weekend in December. It is a tradition we started the first year we lived here because everyone wanted to see the new place, and finding it was a great way to visit with a lot of the friends and family we didn't get to see often we have continued it. My mother had passed away the year before, so to honour her love of the Christmas season we prepared her favourite foods and hosted the event in her memory. I also encourage anyone who plays a musical instrument to bring it so we can wind up the evening with a good old-fashioned carol sing-along. Everyone seems to love the good food and the chance to visit and the event has grown each year until in recent years we have had as many as sixty five people gather.

The first year, 2001, a friend of the family brought me a housewarming/Christmas gift: a large, fancy jar of multicoloured pasta. After the pasta had been eaten, the empty jar sat on my cupboard. I moved it from one spot to the other in my kitchen, but I had never filled it again or found a permanent home for it.

Early in November 2004, Jill and I went into a house cleaning frenzy in preparation for the Christmas season. We washed cookie cans and rearranged the cupboards so they would be ready to receive the plethora of Christmas baking I produced and party supplies we would buy. When I got to the pantry, there was "the jar," still empty and looking dejected. It really should not have presented such a problem for me, but that jar seemed to have a special personality, much like the gentleman who had presented it to me. I know this sounds strange, but it was as if that jar needed to be recognized with something special to fill it. Well, in my haste to make order of my cupboards, I grabbed a large bag of common navy beans, thinking that the jar was an ideal way to store them. They fit perfectly, and I thought I was quite clever as I shoved it back into the pantry alongside the other jars containing oatmeal and nuts that sat beside the boxes of crackers and other dry goods.

However, that decision came back to haunt me on that fateful evening when I went looking for a late-night snack of soda crackers to quell an upset tummy. I opened the pantry door, reached in for the crackers, and was surprised to find the little jar hopping out of the cupboard as if it had grown legs. It landed at my feet with a crash, sending shards of glass and little navy beans to the four corners of the kitchen and beyond.

After recovering from the initial shock, I was dismayed at the amount of time cleaning up the beans and glass would take. Navy beans roll every which way because of their shape and when mixed with sharp little shards of glass become almost as impossible to corral as my old friend Ninny and her cohorts were years ago. I had been counting on a quiet half hour to relax with a cup of tea and do some reading before I went to sleep. As I began to push the beans together, their uncooperative way of rolling across the kitchen tiles reminded me so much of the frustration of running after the cows back on the farm that I was glad we didn't own any cows. As I continued the cleanup, I had a "bean-enforced time of reflection." I thought of how much time we waste chasing the Ninny's or "herding the beans" of our lives and sarcastically asked in a quiet voice, "Now what am I supposed to learn from this?" The answer came to my mind, "Patience, meekness, and long-suffering in times of trouble!" God's voice seemed to ring in the stillness of my kitchen as I picked up broken glass and chased beans from under furniture and inside the front hall closet toward the dustpan. I determined right there and then to plan and do things more carefully in future and to have more patience. That commitment was, however, soon to be put to the test.

You see, I began to write this piece for a Sunday service for which I had been asked to share a testimony. I felt there was a potential lesson from the jar that had fallen, or rather "hopped," out of the cupboard and the spilled beans, but I could not seem to end the piece with an inspiring message. Then, one year later, I understood why. The message was still to be revealed.

Our family had to contend with six or seven different problems that distracted me from what I had hoped to achieve and wasted a lot of precious time all in the one week. While one of our employees was off on vacation, another smashed his thumb in the van door, rendering him unable to handle clothing. Then my son had a car accident, and the steam boiler acted up. We had to find clothing that had been misplaced, and last but not least, just to finish the week off with a bang, someone broke into our dry cleaning store by drilling through the lock on the front door. I received a call from the police at 1:30 a.m. on Thursday and went to find that the thieves had made off with about twenty thousand dollars in merchandise, including wedding gowns, fancy women's clothing and suits. They left a huge mess when they dumped the drawers of my desk and I felt overwhelmed as I faced the horrendous task of cleaning up and informing our clientele of the theft.

At two in the morning, as I began to pick up the pieces of our business and do a physical inventory that I knew the insurance company would need, I felt once more the frustration of wasted time. While picking up scattered invoices and clothing, I remembered running after that uncooperative cow, Ninny, as well as the many times I had wasted time herding the "beans" of my life. I recalled the wasted years after I was divorced from my first husband when I was so depressed that I was barely able to function as a parent, much less continue as a Sunday school teacher. So there among the spilled papers and messed-up clothing, I had a little talk with God. "Ah, ha!" I said. "I understand now. That other stuff was training, wasn't it? All that running after cows and sweeping up the spilled beans were training exercises! So what else is there in my future that I will have to contend with?"

In the stillness of that late night hour, I asked God to help me cope with the problems of life while I continued to clean up. I realized it was of no use to worry about what had happened in the past or may happen in the future because there will always be cows to chase or "spilled beans" to herd. I also realized that it really is not about herding the "beans," but rather it is about the lessons we learn from the event and how we handle adversity. I remembered what God tells us in Joel 2:25-28:

> I will repay you for the years the locusts have eaten—the great locust and the young locust, the flying locust and the locust swarm—my great army I sent among you. You will have plenty to eat, until

you are full, and you will praise the name of the Lord
your God, who has worked wonders for you.

This was a verse our pastor, Pat, had shared with me
shortly before this event had occurred, encouraging me to
leave the past behind and move forward.

I made up my mind right there and then that I would not
waste any more time worrying. I asked God, there among the
mess, to help me make up for the wasted years and focus
instead on what is truly important and to allow me to serve
Him once more, wherever He wanted, in whatever capacity
he wanted.

The next day, my Bible study included Matthew 6, where,
in verse 34, Christ tells us, "Therefore, do not worry about
tomorrow, for tomorrow will worry about itself. Each day has
enough trouble of its own."

Soon after, when I shared this story to my friend, he said,
"It seems the Evil One becomes very jealous if we spend time
serving God, and he finds ways to distract us from our good
intentions."

I agree. So watch out for "spilled beans" in your life if you
have made a commitment to serve God!

Turn Your Radio On

During the 1950s, before I started school, we did not have access to electricity or telephone on our farm, and neither did any of our neighbors. To experience either of these phenomena, one had to drive to the sleepy little town of Golden Prairie, so named because the prairie was golden from lack of rain or snow most months of the year. The town, located near the Greater Sand Hills seven and a half miles away from our farm, had electricity, but only during peak hours by a generator, whose operator went off duty at 9:30 p.m. I swear they rolled up the streets and put them away at about the same time because nothing much happened in town after that.

If we wanted to contact anyone by telephone, we had to drive to Golden Prairie, where the only public phone was in the general store. Then you would have to ring up the central operator, who would connect you to another operator at the local exchange, who would eventually connect you to the number you were trying to reach. Describing this whole process reminds me of the skit on *The Smothers Brothers Show* in the 1960s, in which Lily Tomlin played Ernestine, the telephone operator. Wearing her headset and managing the many plugs for the switchboard, she said her famous line, "One ringy dingy, two ringy dingies." Then when the person answered, she would ask, "Is this the party to whom I am speaking?"

Most phone lines in rural communities were party lines in those days, and Ernestine's question, although humorous, may have been more appropriate than we thought. A party line meant that perhaps ten homes might be on the same telephone line, which meant that any or all of those ten people could listen in on your call, with some even having the audacity to make comments during your conversation. My aunt's phone number was three long rings and two short ones, but that distinguished ring didn't mean she would be the only one who lifted her receiver when it was heard. Because there wasn't much entertainment in those days, listening in on other people was an irresistible temptation. This practice made everyone wary of what was said, and callers soon learned not to say anything they didn't want to become common knowledge in the surrounding community. In fact, particularly juicy bits of conversations were often published in the local newspaper!

And speaking of newspapers, we received only two: the local *Maple Creek News* and the *Winnipeg Free Press*. The *Winnipeg Free Press* contained editorials usually about politics, recipes, weather predictions, cattle and grain prices, as well as stories known as *The Adventures of Reddy Fox* by Thornton W. Burgess and the comics, which I loved. The *Maple Creek News* published a report from each little town within a hundred miles of the paper's office. For this, the editor would choose a reporter from each town who was responsible for gathering and submitting the news to be published in the paper. These papers had little value except for the classifieds and reports of the dates of local events, such as auction sales, baseball games, or curling bonspiels. Other than that, the "news" was largely comprised of gossip, such as who had motored to the city to visit relatives, or notices, such as, "So-and-So's cow was lost. Could you please inform him (her) if you saw said cow?" Announcements about showers for the bride-elect of Mr. So-and-So were highlights for the local women, as were the lengthy descriptions and details of the wedding ceremony, reception, and honeymoon of the latest couple wed. There might even be a picture of the honoured bride and groom for all the young girls to drool over. In the small towns of Saskatchewan, there wasn't much happening, so everyone soon learned to keep their mouth shut when in the company of the "reporter" lest you find your words in print the next mail day.

That being said, mail was moved by train, along with machine parts, baby chicks, fresh fruit, and groceries. Parcels from the Eaton's catalogue and the mail were delivered on Thursdays at the local post office where everyone rented a box. Why Thursday? Because the train came on Wednesday, and it took the mailman some time to sort. So the next day, when the mail was available, the town bustled with activity as people came from miles around to shop, gather their mail, and visit. People would visit in the post office, on the street corners, or in the grocery store, sharing news of older children who had left home to work in the city and general news of the health and welfare of their extended families.

While they visited, people shopped for those items they could not grow themselves. The general store was a treasure trove of unusual articles, selling things such as shoes, lamps, jewelry, nails by the pound, and tools, as well as groceries. There were always fresh eggs from a local farmer, a large, covered wheel of cheese on the counter, and sausages on hooks, as well as exotic foods imported from faraway places. Women could buy fabric and redeem the coupons from The Blue Ribbon products they faithfully bought for things like china with the Prairie Rose pattern, while we children coveted the toys on the top shelf and the candy in the jars on the counter.

Other than the excitement of seeing friends on mail days, there was little entertainment. There were the church concerts, potluck suppers, school concerts, and the occasional dance at the community hall on Saturday nights, which we, being Baptist, were not allowed to attend. Sporting events consisted of the endless and very competitive baseball tournaments in summer and the curling bonspiels in winter, but other than the entertainment people provided for themselves, like meeting to play cards or music, there was little excitement. There was a pool hall that my parents frowned upon, but we did not have movies or bowling, and even after television became available, you could still only watch it until the electricity went off at 9:30.

Not having electricity meant various other things as well. For one thing, you did not have a flush toilet or running water. I joke that we did, however, have "running" water on our farm because my mother was famous for saying to the nearest person who was not gainfully employed in some other chore, "Please run! Get a pail of water." The delights of the outhouse remained, though, right up to when Mom and Dad retired from the farm in 1968. We were always searching for pages out of magazines and old catalogues that were soft enough to use as toilet paper. I remember the orange wrappers that came with the Christmas oranges with *real* fondness.

Not having electricity also meant Dad had to drain all the oil out of the old farm truck and remove the battery the night before we planned to go to town on those cold days around Christmas to shop for the aforementioned oranges. He would bring the battery and oil into the house to warm up behind the stove because there was no block heater, and even if there had been, there was no electrical outlet to plug it into. I never really appreciated the amount of time and effort my father put into making sure I was able to go to youth meetings at church, school concerts, or the skating rink so I could be with my friends until I was thirty-something with two children of my own who needed to go places on winter evenings. On one of those cold evenings, when I sat waiting for one of my children outside the school, the immensity of his dedication suddenly struck me, and I said a tearful prayer of thanks for the father I had been blessed with.

Not having electricity also meant you worked after dark by the light of a coal oil lamp or the much-improved, high-test gasoline lamp, which functioned much like the Coleman lanterns used for camping these days. It had mantels that had to be guarded against flying insects, as they were fragile. Even moving the lamp to pump up the gas tank could destroy them. That being said, the pressurized tank had to be pumped up with air regularly if you wanted the lamp to continue burning brightly, as the light dimmed as the gas level diminished.

Not having electricity meant you had a coal and woodstove in the kitchen, which further meant you had to have a steady supply of wood that had to be cut and hauled in from a great distance or salvaged from old fence posts or coal that was brought to town by train. Wood being hard to come by and coal being very expensive caused the farm people to revert to using what one old timer called "grasoline," a polite term for dried cow dung. The cow paddies were cheap, requiring only an investment of time to walk the pasture to collect them and in plentiful supply when you owned a herd of cattle. My parents used "cow chips" as an alternate fuel for years until a shiny, white propane cook stove became our mother's pride and joy when propane became available in tanks.

Not having electricity meant that there were no refrigerators, so milk was kept cool by hanging it in the well and meat was canned in jars or smoked and cured. Ice cream was a special treat you might get if you behaved particularly well when you went to town for the mail or if your parents went to the trouble of making some when company came. I remember turning and turning the ice cream maker or, in our case, a big syrup pail set in a bucket of ice and salt until the delicious mixture of real cream, eggs, and sugar was frozen enough to serve. To this day, ice cream remains the ultimate treat for me!

Not having electricity also meant you did not have television even after people in town were able to receive the signal—as long as the generator was on, that is. I remember the townspeople petitioning the generator operator to keep it running for an extra hour or two on weekends so they could watch *Country Hoedown* on Friday nights, *Dragnet*, *Gunsmoke*, or *I Love Lucy* on Saturday, *Bonanza* and *The Ed Sullivan Show* finishing off the weekend on Sunday nights. However, on the farm, our entertainment was still comprised of reading, board games, and listening to the radio.

Radio was probably the single most important develop-
ment for the scattered homes and towns across the prairies.
Marconi was given a patent for
the invention of the radio in 1904,
and after that, the miracle of radio
communication spread across
North America. Radio then came
to the prairies about 1922 and
became a window to the world
for the homes scattered in remote
communities.

Our radio, built by Marconi
was a wooden console with a
tuning dial and volume button
on the front, and the back had
a magnificent array of wires
and tubes that lit up. I was only
allowed to observe from a distance when it was hooked to a
large battery, its power source that was not used frivolously
in those days, as batteries were expensive and we did not
have much money for luxuries. The receiver worked very well,
even bringing radio broadcasts from foreign countries into
our house because my father and brother had erected a long
aerial that ran from the radio through the window frame, up
the outside of the house to the highest point, and across the
yard at least a hundred feet to the peak of Dad's shop. We
then heard radio broadcasts from Russia, Mexico, and cities
all over the United States.

A favourite program I listened to late at night was "Hawaii
Calls" which came to us from the Royal Hawaiian Hotel on
Waikiki Beach. It was my introduction to the dulcet tones of
the ukulele and the Hawaiian singers with the sound of the
ocean waves as back up.

The Canadian Broadcasting Corporation had come into
existence in 1936 and soon became the mainstay of listening
pleasure in our house. I learned at a very early age to be

very quiet while my father listened to the news and market reports—not the stock market but reports about the price of grain, cattle, and hogs. I still enjoy listening to those reports today on the country stations in our area. In those days, Dad would sit with an ear near the radio first thing in the morning and again at noon when he came in for lunch, giving it his complete attention. The announcer would provide us with local news and reports from around the world. Local weather reports as well the latest market prices would help Dad to decide which grain to plant and when to sell it, whether to breed more hogs or stick with cattle.

In the afternoon, there would also be some form of entertainment. Soap opera's like *Fibber McGee and Molly, Our Miss Brooks*, and stories like *Jake and the Kid* by our very own home-grown author, W. O. Mitchell came on soon after the noon news. These stories entertained us while we paused for the noon meal, and listening to these characters' antics was a welcome distraction and a good excuse to rest from the hard work of farming.

Radio provided all the entertainment a busy farm family had time for, with the evening fare of the *Wayne and Schuster Comedy Hour* or *Rawhide* giving comic relief to the serious business of survival on the prairies. Dramas like *The Lone Ranger* with his sidekick Tonto and *The Cisco Kid* with Poncho kept us on the edge of our seats as they fought for truth and honour. Then Saturday night was hockey night in Canada. Again, I learned to play very quietly while the family listened with bated breath to the play-by-play with Foster Hewitt.

On Saturday afternoon, I often went to sleep to the strains of the Metropolitan Opera sponsored by Texaco. My brother was an avid listener, and from this, I learned to love the characters portrayed in the unusual musical stories and the events of their lives sung by the most famous operatic voices of that time. As I grew older and after my brother left home, I still listened to the opera as I did my housework, and to the consternation of our neighbor who lived five miles away, I learned to mimic those arias and sang them while fetching the cows from the pasture. He often exclaimed over my ability to project my voice as he could hear me singing over the five miles of prairie that separated our farm from his.

On Sunday, there was always a Christian broadcast or two that was our only church service if we were snowed in or encouraged us while we got ready to attend the tiny church in town in summer. I remember the *Back to the Bible Broadcast* with Theodore H. Epp and a children's broadcast called *The Adventures of Danny Orlis* that contained stories about the adventures of a boy and his friends who lived near Lake of the Woods. Ernest Manning was my Dad's favourite, as he delivered Bible-based dissertations on *Canada's National Bible Hour*. These Bible teachers were really excited about their radio broadcasts, believing this form of media would allow them to reach many more people with the gospel. They often quoted Mark 16:15: "He said unto them, 'Go into all the world and preach the good news to all creation,'" and say that they were now able to cross borders with their broadcasts that had been closed to them before. Those broadcasts are still on sixty years later and reach millions with the message of Christ everyday.

The radio was my introduction to the art of storytelling with its many broadcasts about people in distant places and events from around the world. I would sit glued to the radio as a teenager and would still today rather listen to the radio than watch movies or television. I find it leaves your hands and eyes free to do other things, not to mention it allows your imagination free reign to visualize the hero and heroine as the plot of a radio drama unfolds. Tune in for the next episode.

A Tribute to Those Who Came Before

While at a Bible study, a group of friends and I were discussing the people who had influenced and possibly even changed the course of history for our families. As a result of that discussion, I wrote this tribute to Grandma and Grandpa Frank, who lived and practiced their faith throughout their lives.

Grandma and Grandpa immigrated to Canada from Romania in 1913. The journey had begun two years earlier with a discussion about the political climate in Eastern Europe. In 1911, they, along with other German-speaking friends of the same faith in their small community, decided to leave what seemed like a hopeless situation. They had seen the posters offering land and a new life in America. By leaving Europe, they escaped the horrors of World War I and all the mayhem that followed. As a result, my ten uncles avoided fighting in what Grandpa called "that useless war." However, two of the younger boys went to fight for the allied nations in World War II.

Grandma and Grandpa had twenty-one children. Three died in infancy, one daughter stayed behind in Europe with her husband and infant son, and their eldest son immigrated to Argentina, but the rest came with their parents and survived to become good, hardworking citizens in their new home. They arrived in the New World on April 19, 1913, at Portland, Maine. Their travels from there to their eventual home in Saskatchewan are lost in the annals of time, but we do know that they travelled by train across Canada. I can't imagine undertaking that trip with so many children even with modern transportation, much less travelling steerage on a steamboat across the Atlantic and then across Canada in railcars not much better than boxcars.

Although they were poor, I believe Grandma and Grandpa had a dream of a better life that helped them endure the hardships of that arduous trip. No matter what motivated them, it still took heroic bravery and internal fortitude to make that voyage. When they arrived in Maple Creek, Saskatchewan, the summer was already upon them, and they still had to travel about forty or fifty miles across the open prairie to the land they were given to homestead. My dad spoke often of walking beside the wagon across the plains for many miles and the relief when they found the survey markers for their land, indicating that their long journey had ended.

The land was comprised of gently rolling hills devoid of vegetation except for prairie grass, herbs like wild onions and sage, wild roses, cactus, and a few chokecherry and Saskatoon bushes. There were plenty of deer and antelope in the sand hills nearby, but the buffalo had pretty well disappeared from the prairies by the time they arrived having been hunted to near extinction by the white settlers by that time.

My father, who was eleven when they arrived, said their first job was to build a shelter against the winter that was fast approaching. They dug a deep trench about ten feet wide by ten feet deep into the side of one of the highest hills on their property. Then they dismantled the wagon box for its lumber, which they used to make a roof, topping it off with a layer of sod blocks cut from the prairie close by. The following year they built a real "soddy," so  called because it was constructed entirely out of blocks of sod measuring ten by twenty inches. It had three rooms and a chimney for the cook stove.

I have a picture of Grandma and Grandpa in front of their first real wooden house in which my grandfather is holding up an open Bible. I wish I knew what chapter and verse he found to sustain them during this epic journey and the hard

work it took to fulfill the terms of the contract he had signed with the Government of Canada. The contract said they must break eighteen acres and plant a crop the first year. I have the documents proving they achieved this using a one-bottom plow and many hours of hoeing. They lived in that soddy for two years before they had assembled enough materials to build that wooden house.

Once in my teens, I had the thrill of visiting the site of their first home in Canada. It seemed to me that I could still feel their presence there even though they had been gone for over sixty years. As I stood in the ruins of the soddy, looking across the prairies toward the Big Stick Lake, the only large body of water nearby, I imagined what it must have been like for them to leave family and friends in a beautiful homeland to come to this desolate landscape. But I know it was their dream and determination to have a better life that laid the foundation for this country and the life style our family enjoys today.

They raised and homeschooled their children on that small homestead farm in southern Saskatchewan. They had very few books aside from the Bible and one called *The Living Oak*, which was a book of stories containing a life, or moral, lesson. Dad said Grandpa was very strict and would not let them leave their lessons for play until they had memorized at least three Bible verses, read something out loud, and had done some basic math. His discipline and teaching stood them in good stead as most of them were able to read documents and books as well as perform basic math in their adult years.

I remember my aunts, uncles, and cousins as artistic, hardworking, and self-sufficient. My uncles were farmers, mechanics, and carpenters, skills I'm sure they learned from Grandpa who was a skilled wheelwright and carpenter as well as a farmer. The girls learned to cook, bake, and sew from Grandma and raised large families of their own, passing on those skills. They also passed on their deep, abiding faith in God, which still sustains our generation.

The community in which they lived seemed to have made the decision to immigrate to Canada en mass, so the settlement here was comprised of other families with a similar background who knew and helped each other. They brought with them their traditions of hard work and faith and so banded together to build roads, schools, and a little church called Rosenfeld, so named because of the wild roses that grew in the churchyard. Grandpa was known in the congregation as a Bible scholar and was soon elected lay pastor until they found a pastor from a seminary.

Born in 1865, Grandma, who was a midwife as well as a wife, mother and formidable homemaker, knew how to treat illness using herbs. They arrived in this country at a time when there were few conveniences to aid her in her daily chores. She did laundry with homemade lye soap and a washboard in a washtub and sewed clothing for her large family by hand. She was famous for her home-baked bread and tasty stew, which she offered to all who came her way. Dad used to say Grandma could make good soup even if all she had for ingredients were rusty nails. She often quoted, "Cleanliness is next to godliness" to her children, and I don't even want to think about the effort it took to keep all those children clean and fed in those primitive conditions.

After Grandpa passed away, Grandma came to live with my mother and father. Although she passed away before I was born, Mom, who loved her, remembered her loving service to the family as she told Bible stories, baked, helped to prepare meals, and work in the garden. She truly had a servant's heart.

At age seventy-seven, in the fall of 1943, Grandma was pulling weeds and vegetables in the garden. Feeling sorry for the pigs that were penned in a corral with nothing green to eat, she gathered as many of the green vegetable tops and weeds she could carry in her big, white apron and offered them to the animals. After this long walk, she told Dad she was tired and went into the house to take a nap. Grandma never woke from that nap but went home to be with her Lord, who had been her strength and whose teachings were the foundation for her life of service.

My father told me she often quoted, "I can do all things through Christ who strengthens me" in her native German language. I have also come to love the same verse:

> I know what it is to be in need, and I know what it is to have plenty. I have learned the secret of being content in any and every situation, whether well fed Or hungry, whether living in plenty or in want. I can do all things through Him who strengthens me (Philippians 4:12, 13).

Although I didn't get to know my grandparents as they passed away before I was born so, I am thankful for their faith and hard work that my father spoke of and practiced himself. I know what they did changed the course of my life and that of our family forever.

I travelled to their homeland in Romania last year, the one hundredth anniversary of their decision to leave, and saw for myself the home and village they had left behind. As I sat on the banks of the beautiful blue Danube overlooking the lush fields of the Dobrajan Plain and the forest nearby, which are such a sharp contrast to the windswept sand hills of Saskatchewan, the immensity of their sacrifice struck me. I shed unabashed tears as I marveled at the courage that brought them from the beauty and security of that faraway land to the uncertain future in a "soddy" on the prairies.

Many times I have sent up a prayer of thanks for the sacrifice my grandparents made, especially when I hear stories of the adversities faced by those who chose to stay in Europe. I have come to believe that my grandparents were given divine guidance and am thankful for their God-given foresight and faith that sustained them and their family as they made the trek to this wonderful land, Canada, which my children and I now call home.

Berry Pickers

"George, wait for me!" August shouted, pulling on his jacket.

"Me too. Me too! I want to come with you!" Sarah insisted.

"Girls are too slow. We guys are running fast, Sarah!" With that, August and George ran off.

"Boys! Boys! Come back!" Mother shouted from the doorway of the little sod house. "If you think you can just run off to play, you are wrong! The Saskatoon's are ripe out by the pasture, and I want you to pick as many as you can before noon *and*," she drew herself up to her full five feet, "you take Sarah along so she can help you pick!"

"She's too slow!" groaned the boys in unison.

"This isn't about being fast!" Mother insisted. "I want lots of nice, juicy berries in the bucket, not a bunch of leaves and twigs. And don't squash them! I want to preserve them, not make them into jam."

The two boys groaned again but obediently picked up the two milk pails standing by the stove, while their sister Sarah pulled down the big, blue enamel stew pot from the shelf. With that, this ragtag little band set off across the prairie, pails clanking, toward the bluff of Saskatoon bushes on the far side of the pasture. They raced when they were about halfway there and ran like the wind, bare feet barely touching the prairie wool as they went. The soles of their feet were so callused from going barefooted all summer that they hardly felt the small pebbles and cactus thorns.

"I win, I win!" yelled August as he reached the post that marked the end of the pasture. "I get to choose the first piece of johnnycake!"

"Not fair!" protested Sarah. "I'm the girl. I should get first pick!" So the battle raged between the three siblings, who were more like triplets having been born within a year of each other, as they began to pick the luscious berries. These berries, the only fresh fruit worth preserving in this part of the country, grew wild and made a sweet treat for them when winter settled in. They knew just how cold it could get when the winter winds blew over the Canadian plains, and being in their early teens, they were old enough to understand that they

must help gather as much food as they could while it was available. With a family of sixteen to feed, there was little time for relaxing and none for fooling around.

The three split up, each taking a different bush and stripping the branches bare in record time. However, over the next two hours that it took to fill the buckets, the three mouths also found their fair share of berries, turning their lips purple. When their buckets were full, they stopped for their lunch of johnnycake and homemade cheese.

George ate his portion quickly and lay back on the sandy cut-bank to watch the clouds sailing overhead. "I see a horse with a wolf chasing it!" He called to the others.

Sarah joined the game. "I see a princess in a ball gown."

"Oh pooh, you always see princesses. You have such an imagination!"

"Well, I did see a princess when the archduke came to town when we were still back home. She was beautiful in her satin gown!"

"That was then, and this is now!" George, the serious one, barked. He missed the country they had come from, and one day, he promised himself, he would return to live there, where the soil was rich and fruit like peaches grew wild. He missed going on fishing trips with his father and the other boys to the Danube River.

George knew that his mother missed the beautiful house she had left behind because he heard her talk of it to her friend and saw tears drip down her round, rosy cheeks. His father missed the way of life they once had, but war was raging in Europe now. Ever since Archduke Ferdinand had been shot and all the countries of Europe were being forced to take sides and fight in what Father called "that useless war," George understood that his older brothers would have been forced to join the army even though they were young, so he knew they were better off here. But it was hard living on this dry, open plain when he was used to trees and good food from that farm so far away.

Shaking himself free of those thoughts, George joked, "I want sheep's cheese on toast for supper." With that, he got up and trudged off, carrying his bucket of berries. August and Sarah guessed that their brother was once more remembering their homeland, and since there was no rich, creamy sheep's cheese because they had no sheep to provide it, they would have to be satisfied with the coarse cottage cheese Mother made out of the cow's milk they did have.

"I see a ship like the one that brought us across the ocean. Just look at it!" August yelled after his brother, trying to cheer him up. He was disappointed that the game had taken on this sour flavour and began climbing the hill behind his brother. "And I see Mother waiting for us on the doorstep!" George yelled back from his vantage point at the top of the hill. "She'll want us to fill the pails again this afternoon, so hurry up!"

Mother was indeed waiting, with jars washed and ready to receive the berries. The sweet smell of the cooking syrup she had prepared greeted them as they handed over the buckets. George had been right about her orders for the afternoon; only, to their satisfaction, she kept Sarah in the house to wash the berries and pick out the green and spoiled ones as well as the leaves that inevitably found their way into the bucket when they were picking fast. This meant they didn't have to wait for their sister or pick the thorns from her much-softer feet.

The boys ran off in a new direction before their mother could stop them. They had been exploring the prairie around their homestead and had found a large bunch of berry bushes about a mile away that was growing out of the side of a sand dune. They climbed the grass-covered slope of the dune, one of the highest points in the surrounding flatland, to survey the countryside. From there, they could see the sand dunes and poplar trees of the semi-desert off to the east, the Big Stick Lake a few miles away, and a herd of antelope quietly grazing about a half mile away. The midday sun was still hot for late September, and they knew their father would not hunt for the winter supply of meat until it cooled off in November, but a fresh steak or roast would be really tasty right now. They determined to tell him about this herd when he came home from his trip to Fox Valley, the little town to the north. They slid down the steep side of the dune and began picking berries with real ambition, as they knew they could take a few minutes to explore a little farther if they were quick at their work. When the berry buckets were filled, they set them in the shade and raced to the next row of dunes a few yards away. Again they climbed the grassy side and slid down the steep side, this time getting sand up their pant legs and hopping up and down to shake it out. There were no Saskatoon berry bushes here, but there were a few chokecherries, and they loved the jam Mother made from those berries. The two boys walked around the bushes, tasting the ripe fruit that made their teeth feel funny and was really sour. But it became a tasty treat when cooked with a lot of sugar and mixed with a little sweet cream or poured over ice cream.

"We'll tell Mom, and come back tomorrow," August said from his side of the bush, but he heard no answer. When he came around the bush, he found George frozen in place, facing off with the biggest badger he had ever seen. August picked up a large branch lying nearby and, yelling with all his might, ran at the badger.

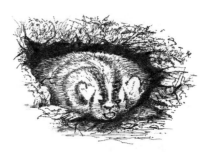

Badgers are big and ferocious, and the boys knew this one could attack them at any moment and do real damage if they didn't get it to back down or if they didn't get away. "Back up real slow so you're behind me," August instructed his shaking brother. "I have a big stick, so I can hit him if he attacks." He sounded braver than he felt.

They both backed away slowly, allowing the badger enough space to feel secure, before they turned tail and scrambled up the steep embankment on all fours as fast as their hands and feet could carry them. Still shaking, they retrieved the two pails of berries and planned how they would tell their father about the badger while they made their way home. The family supplemented their meager income by catching fur-bearing animals in the winter and knew that badgers were prized for their fur. The traders would pay a handsome price for one that was so large and in prime condition.

That evening when Father returned and the chores were done, the boys told their tale of adventure and discovery to the whole family as they sat around the kitchen table eating the last of a Saskatoon pie Mother had made in honour of Father's return.

"He was *this big*!" George spread his hands at least three feet apart. "And I was as close to him as I am to you."

"You should take better care when you're out there! You could have been badly injured if he had attacked," Father scolded.

George hung his head. "But, Dad, I know we can snare him and get a good price for the fur."

"Well, I'll go with you to see this big badger, but we should wait until later in the fall to catch him because his fur will grow in thicker after the cold wind starts to blow."

The wood in the stove crackled just then, sending a shower of sparks up the chimney, reminding them that the day was done and they had better get to bed. The work of preparing for winter would be waiting for them again as the sun came up. Father reached for the big, old German Bible that a dying soldier had given him back in their homeland to read a Psalm, which was his custom every evening before they blew out the lamp. Tonight, it was Psalm 122: 1-8. They listened to as he solemnly read:

> I lift up my eyes to the hills—where does my help
> come from?
> My help comes from the Lord, the Maker of heaven
> and earth.
> He will not let your foot slip—he who watches over
> you will not slumber;
> Indeed, he who watches over Israel will neither
> slumber nor sleep.
> The Lord watches over you—the Lord is your shade
> at your right hand.
> The sun will not harm you by day, or the moon by
> night.
> The Lord will keep you from all harm—he will watch
> over your life;
> The Lord will watch over your coming and going
> both now and forevermore.

So reassured by God's Word, the children went off to a good night's sleep.

Some forty-two years later, George and August planned a day of berry picking back in the sand hills near where they had spent the first few years of their life in Canada. Their two families would pick berries, and they would tell the stories to their children of those days long ago while visiting in the shade of the big, old Russian poplar trees that grew in the low places. They loaded milk pails, cream cans, and boxes to hold the bountiful berries they were sure they would find. Their wives, Molly and Julia, had packed enough food to feed an army along with jars of sweet coffee and tea. The army, their ten children, climbed into the back of the farm trucks along with the pails and lunch boxes to sing and laugh their way across the wild terrain, past Grant's sheep farm, and out into the dunes, where antelope herds still raced alongside the passing vehicles and badgers still dug burrows into the lee side of the hills.

God's Cure for Boredom

Now gather around, and I'll tell you a story,
About my dear dad, who's gone on to glory.
This story's been told so many times,
But only this year, I've put it in rhymes.

It involves the pig Gertrude, who became a real pet,
And the cow Daisy, whose ways were quite set.
Dear dad was a farmer, a fine example of love.
He believed every creature was sent from above.
He reminded us often that God watched all our ways,
"Accountable," he said, "God will hold us each day.
We are the masters while here on Earth,
And by all our actions, He'll measure our worth.
God will encourage each horse at the plow.
And for her great bounty, he'll love every cow.
Dogs are so loyal, loving, and true,
If man is unkind, that day he will rue!
Chickens as well have a place in God's plan
For they all resemble the family of man."

So out on our farm all the creatures had names.
Each got a pat and joined in his games.
"Do unto others" was how Dad lived his life.
That's how he treated beast, neighbor, and wife.

Gertrude the pig was tiny at birth.
Dad gave her to me; she wasn't much worth.
But fed bottles by hand and kept like a pet,
She soon realized that for life she was set.

No gate kept her in, for she could unlock it.
She'd sit for a scratch or a treat from my pocket.
The mat by the door with the dog she would share
And soon we were used to finding her there.
She played in the yard and soon caught a ball.
But Dad said, "She's full grown and must go to a stall."
So he built a new barn with a floor of cement.
Her attempts to escape this would prevent.
Soon she was settled and became a fine mother,
Her litters were large, which delighted my brother.
Pork prices were high, and so we made money.
I was real proud, and called her "my honey."

Our farm was no ranch, just a section and a half,
So Dad had the time to tend every calf.
But one was so special and had so much charm,
We watched over her so she'd come to no harm.
Then she learned to slip fences as easy as pie.
She ate all the daisies and made my mom cry.
Eating the daisies became her claim to fame,
So raiding Mom's garden gave Daisy her name.
With curly, white face and the rest chocolate brown,
She won many ribbons at the fair in our town.
She'd bat her long lashes and moo at my Dad;
She looked like a picture from a magazine ad.

When I came to the barn my dad was real strict.
I had to sit high so I wouldn't get kicked.
I'd watch from my perch way up in the loft
The kittens were there, and the hay was real soft.
Each cow had her place and each had her pail.
Each had her own space to come to the rail.
Ninny would kick and roll her big eyes.
Nelly would snort and heave such big sighs.
Bossy would bunt and shove for more space.
But Daisy was calm and came straight to her place.

Before they were milked, they were given some chop
A little ground oats with molasses on top.
Dad was so fussy, he cleaned every udder.
That tickled, I guess, for it made Daisy shudder.
Then she would shake and give a great cough,
The chickens would cackle and then they'd take off.

The scene is now set. It was a cold day in November,
A much colder day than Dad or Mom could remember.
Dad came in real late to sit down and eat,
The dog came in too to sit at his feet.
"This dog is my pal, but he usually stays out.
A storm is a-brewin', of this there's no doubt!
Today was so warm, but the wind it has turned."
With weather so cold, Dad was concerned
Especially for Gerty, sleeping out in her barn.
She lived there alone, and it was hard to keep warm.
Again out he went, with a rope and a light.
To find a solution to Gerty's cold plight.
He led her along to a much warmer bed,
He'd give her a place right in the cowshed.
The cow in one stall, the pig in another,
Just like old Noah's Ark, each slept by the other.
The cat was curled up in the hay in the loft
And the dog was down there with a blanket so soft
The chickens were roosting way up in the rafters.
Their clucking, well, it sounded a little like laughter.
Maybe that sound was an omen or warning,
Of what would take place right there the next morning.

Next morning dawned bright and all was aglitter,
For there was a new frost on each leaf and each critter.
The ice it had formed on the trough and the slough,
The golden leaves danced while the autumn wind blew.
At breakfast my parents, they were conversing,
Deciding their roles they could be reversing.

Today, she was thinking, she would can pears.
Preserves were so great; she was proud of her wares.
Dad had more time now that harvest was done,
So he'd help with the milking and errands to run.
He dressed up real warm in a jacket and sweater,
To fend off the cold; that made him feel better!
First to the shop for hammer and nails,
Then to the milk house for two clanging pails.

I followed my dad and watched while he worked.
He never was lazy, no duty he'd shirk.
But I felt a change and unrest on that day
As we brought those cows in and spread some new hay.
My dad was quite surly and very short-tempered
He yelled at the cows like I never remembered.
I could not understand his mood or the reason,
So I chalked it all up to the change of the season.
But I was so young and just had to query,
"Do you feel sick or have some cause for worry?"
"Silence is golden!" was all he would say.
"Now go on up to the hayloft to play!"
But as my Dad started to work at his tasks,
I overheard him and the prayers that he asked:

"Oh, my dear Lord, please answer, please.
Why this milk pail here between my old knees?
What value this, to milk this old cow?
Or simply just now, to feed this brood sow?
What good am I doing here on this poor farm?
I'd like to be some place where the temperature's warm!
What a great missionary for You I could be,
If from all these chores, I could be set free.
Just think what I'd do in a mission for others
If I could work elsewhere among my dear brothers.
I'd preach such a sermon for dear Jesus' sake
If I could just leave that old hoe and my rake.

39

Realize, my dear Lord, I'm not really complaining,
It's just that for higher things I am aiming.
But please don't misunderstand me, Lord,
I think I'm just a little bored."

Now, I've heard tell of those who say:
"Take care what you ask, when daily you pray."
If Dad only knew how his talk of boredom
Would find relief right there that morning.
He would have taken back each word and phrase,
And said, "My mood is all just a passing phase."
You see in the barn, all seemed calm and peaceful
But appearances really can be deceitful!
The barn was so warm and kind of hazy
All the animals there seemed quite lazy!
Daisy was chewing her chop in a daze,
Unconcerned with human ways.

Then . . . Dad reached out to brush her udder
And that made Daisy give a terrible shudder.
This was her way to give you warning,
That she must cough again this morning.
Her sides expanded like heaving bellows,
"Move aside, take care, my dear good fellows!"
Her nostrils flared, the tears did run,
She coughed so loud! It was not fun!
Her cough could cause you mortal danger,
For it blew the chop right from the manger.

Now . . . unbeknownst to man or beast,
The sow last night had had a feast.
She'd had some corn then found her rest.
With bed of hay, she had been blessed.
While Dad thought she was in her stall,
She really wasn't there at all!

Her stall had been for her too hard
And it was cold out in the yard.
So she had snuggled in hay so deep,
With no one there to disturb her sleep.
Hidden from view under Daisy's manger,
Gerty really couldn't see the danger.

But Daisy's coughing acted like a trigger
The hay began moving; it got bigger and bigger!
Then out shot Gerty just like a rocket
And things fell out of my daddy's pocket
As he backed up and away real quick
So as to avoid good Daisy's kick!
The cat named Toots, waiting to be fed,
Ended up on Daisy's head!
Then Daisy began to dance a nervous jig
And Toots hung on, and her eyes got big!
Then the cat began to yowl,
And the dog outside offered up a terrible howl.
Next the cow stepped in the pail
And then began to swish her tail.
She swatted Dad upside his head,
I even thought he might be dead,
For he had fallen in the stall
He landed hard, against that wall.
Chickens cackled and flew away,
White feathers fell with bits of hay.

All the while, the pig was squealing,
Like she had some very painful feeling.
Round and round she spun about.
Escape, her aim, she must—get—out!
Just then my Mother, hearing all the racket,
Came through the door with flying jacket.
Gerty saw her chance to run.

"Good-bye!" she squealed. "This is no fun!"
Knocking my mom back out the door,
She fled the scene forevermore.

Slowly . . . Mom and Dad got up,
To be inspected by the pup.
As they brushed their clothing off,
Daisy gave one final cough.
At this, the cat did slink away
Not to be seen again that day.
The feathers settled as well as the dust did.
My Mom asked Dad, "Is anything busted?"
"No," Dad said, still rubbing his head.
"But I can't find my glasses. That pig is dead!"
Now Daddy's glasses were special you see,
With wire rims and lenses round as can be.
Two weeks to get new ones, at the very least,
Now Daddy's temper was rising like yeast.
Down on our knees went Mom, Dad, and me.
Searching through hay and all that debris!

Well after an hour, we had to give up.
We finished the milking and Dad fed the pup.
He gave one last look, way up and around,
While I gave one last look down
on the ground.
"I'll have to let Daisy go out for a
drink,
Then search through this straw
once more, I think."
Wiping his brow, Dad said, "Wow,
what a hassle."
And what do you think he saw
there, caught on Daisy's tassel?
Dad's glasses were hooked right
there on her tail,

While we had been searching through manger and bale.
Swinging and swaying with such bovine grace,
The sight of it all relieved Dad's poor, grim face.
He smiled at first then shouted with laughter,
Until we joined in, and it rang through the rafters.

Now I have come to the end of this matter,
So with these last lines, I'll finish this chatter.
When you feel sad and are tempted to grumble,
Remember the prayer I heard my Dad mumble.
God used all those animals, it is my firm belief,
To bring my Dad laughter and give him some relief.
So if you are bored with everyday things,
Remember this story and the humour it brings.
Then go on your way, and give thanks up to heaven,
That creatures like Daisy to us God has given.

A Fowl Experience

My father's farm always reminded me a little of Noah's Ark. We always had a wide variety of animals, including the usual: dogs, cats, cows, horses, pigs, sheep, chickens, ducks, and turkeys, not to mention other varieties that came and went, such as, wild birds rescued from the field, and rabbits saved from the plow. Caring for so many animals required a great deal of patience and time, and there never seemed to be a dull day. Whenever man and beast come into contact, I have found that there is always the possibility of drama, comedy, or tragedy, as recounted in the following three stories.

Trouble in the Hen Yard

The first inkling we had that there might be trouble in the hen yard was when we heard an unusual amount of noise coming from the chicken house at ten o'clock in the morning one fine Saturday in May. The hens were usually busy scratching, eating, and laying eggs by that time of day, but aside from the cackle of a hen when she laid an egg, it was unusual for them to make that much noise.

Mom, poking her head out the kitchen door, said, "There's trouble in the henhouse for sure!" Thinking there might be a predator lurking nearby, she sent Dad out to investigate, as we had coyote, weasels, and the occasional snake on our Saskatchewan farm. There were also hawks overhead that usually sent the hens into paroxysms of cackling or had them scattering and running for shelter.

Dad returned, laughing, and told us that the hens were all up on the roost cackling because there were two young fellows

squabbling with each other. One was a young rooster defending his rights to the flock, while the other was a young turkey gobbler who seemed to have his wires crossed and was battling for male supremacy in the same hen yard. The gobbler had picked a fight with the rooster while ignoring the female turkeys next door. Dad had separated them, chasing that young scallywag back to his own domain, thinking that that would be the end of the matter. We all had a good chuckle and went back to our Saturday chores.

That, however, was *not* the end of the matter. The two pens were divided only by a single stretch of chicken wire, and the two took to taunting each other through the fence. The young gobbler strutted his stuff, tail spread in an admirable fan with wings dragging in the dirt and wattle turning bright red, all the while giving a mighty loud gobbling challenge. We heard him begin the challenge with, "Took, took, took," ending with a most formidable, long gobble. All the while, the rooster strutted back and forth along the other side of the fence, stopping only when he came to the end of the pen with hate in his eye. There he marked his territory with long scratches in the sand and a long, loud, "Cock-a-doodle-doo!" After that, they were at each other every chance they got.

When the grain in the field next to the hen yard had been cut, Dad opened the fence and the birds were allowed to become free range, looking for bugs and grain left in the field after harvest. The chicken hens and turkey hens got on admirably, often chasing the same grasshoppers across the golden stubble, but that was not enough to distract the two young males from their feud. Soon they were involved in such fierce battles that they drew blood.

Dad and Mom were tired of continually separating the two, so they kept one penned up while the other was allowed to forage, but that ended when both discovered they could fly over the fence. Dad said he would like to butcher the young turkey because he seemed to be the more aggressive of the two, but Mom intervened, saying, "That is not going to happen! His destiny is my roaster at Thanksgiving, and that is still a couple of months away."

Soon we all started carrying a broom when we came out to do chores because when they weren't battling each other, they aimed their aggression at anyone else who crossed their path. The dog learned to steer clear, and even the cat ran for cover whenever they were out and about.

One afternoon, Dad was working in the shop when he heard the commotion begin for one more battle round. The chicken and turkey hens began to cackle, and the battle cry was sounded. He looked out in time to see the two circling each other like wrestlers in a ring. Dad reached for the stub of an old corn broom worn down after many years of cleaning up grain in the bins and went out to put an end to their fighting once more.

The battle was into the first round; the two were facing off as he stepped out of the shop. He watched as they did one more circle, and then with the accurate aim of a well-practiced baseball player, he let the broom fly. It flew through the air in a perfect arch and thumped the young turkey in the centre of his pride and joy with a loud whack. The turkey immediately lost his desire to fight and, looking over his shoulder at the young rooster, made tracks for the stubble field. For the rest of that day and well into the next, he walked the perimeter of the field but would not come in even for a drink of water.

Finally, feeling some responsibility, Dad locked the rooster up in the henhouse, fearing the turkey would die of dehydration.

It still took a couple of hours for the gobbler to quietly sneak home, tail down, to take a long drink and duck timidly into the barn where they had been kept as chicks.

After that, the rooster reigned supreme. Every time the gobbler saw the rooster, he headed for the stubble field or hid in the barn. Dad finally came to the conclusion that the gobbler thought that the well-placed whack of the broom must have come from the rooster and so was completely intimidated by his former opponent. The gobbler's sorry existence ended in Mom's roasting pan as a finely dressed bird for Thanksgiving, one of the finest dinners she had ever prepared.

The young rooster with his glossy, black tail and golden plumage became insufferably proud as summer gave way to fall. He would sit on the highest peak of the barn from which his loud reveille woke everyone each morning. With his proud walk and regal air, he watched over his domain and was accepted by one and all as the absolute king of the barnyard.

As Proverbs 22:10 says, "Drive out the mocker, and out goes strife; quarrels and insults are ended." So ends this drama, but the life of the rooster continues into another story of love and defense.

The Great Defender

Every spring, we received a batch of about two to three hundred chicks from the hatchery, where they arrived by train at the station in our little town. We would have to hold them in their crates all the way home so they wouldn't be injured. Once we got them home, our job was to make sure each had a drink and knew how to eat before we put them into the brooder house.

Chicks are a little like human babies and have to be taught survival skills. I loved taking each tiny, yellow chick gently in my hand and, with one finger behind its head, dipping its beak into the water until it took a deep drink, tilting its head back to let the cool water run down its throat for the first time. Then we would spread a small amount of chick starter, a granular food, on a sheet of newspaper on the kitchen table. By tapping on the table with a finger among the grains of food, we encouraged these naturally curious little fellows to try the food. Once they had a taste, they were off and away. This whole process often took until the wee hours of the next morning, when we were all glad to snuggle down for sleep.

Depending on how cold it was outside, to my delight we often kept the little fellows in the house behind the woodstove in the kitchen for a couple of days. They needed to be watched carefully because they tended to all cuddle together in one corner of the crate they had arrived in. This crowding could cause some of them to suffocate, so every hour or so, we had to separate them. Finally, when they were two or three days old, usually about the time they started hopping out of their crate and running every which way in the kitchen, we saw they had become strong enough to defend themselves. We would then carry them to the brooder house, where a heater kept them warm.

By the spring I was six—no, almost seven—Mom felt I was old enough to begin helping with the chores, so she taught me to care for the young chicks and hens. The chicks still needed a lot of care, and it became my job to keep an eye on them. They had to be checked every hour or so, and the water jugs had to be cleaned and refilled as needed. Feeding time was always exciting, and I laughed as the little fellows ran to hide by natural instinct when I made the loud, screeching noise of the hawk. This seemed mean, but they needed to learn that lesson so that a real hawk wouldn't catch them once they were outside. If I brought food, they would come running and peck, often pecking at my toes as well.

In the morning, I was to carry the kitchen scraps to the hen yard and, while the hens ate, gather the eggs. I also learned to pump water into one of the small buckets so I could fill the big, shallow pan Mom had set out for them. In the evening,

I had to make sure that all the chickens were back in their barn and lock the door so they would be safe from predators. Mom warned me every day to watch out for that old rooster, because he did not like anyone setting foot in his territory.

As spring warmed into summer, the new chicks were released into a pen made of chicken wire for the day, and it became my job during summer vacation to watch over, feed, and water them and make sure they all went back into the brooder house at night.

Chickens are great scratchers! They scratch in order to find food. They scratch for exercise, and they scratch deep holes so they can take a dust bath. When one begins to scratch, it usually attracts the attention of at least two or three more who think there may be something delicious there, so they all scratch together. This results in deep holes in the pen. If one of those holes happens to be close to the fence, it can result in the Great Escape, which seemed to be a young chicken's goal and greatest delight but its caretaker's greatest nightmare.

The chickens never strayed too far from their food, but they would hide under machinery during the hot days and in open bins, looking for food. So trying to herd them back into the fence was no easy chore. I usually achieved the roundup by chasing each one until I had it cornered, where I could catch it and return it to the safety of the pen. This was one of those frustrating and time-consuming jobs that resulted in a lot of commotion, cheeping, screeching, and flying feathers as each chick was caught. It also resulted in one very tired, dirty little girl!

One fateful day, I was once again chasing runaways with more than the usual noise, flying feathers, and screeching. As I mentioned before, chickens are naturally curious, and they become more so as they get older. So the older hens and King Rooster came to investigate what all the noise was about.

I had captured all but two escapees when disaster arrived on two large golden wings with black tail feathers and a loud screech. The king of the barnyard had come to defend his chicks. He flew at me with fury, flapping his wings and screeching his objections. With his beak open and talons out, he flew at my face and tore a chunk out of my upper lip, effectively stopping me from capturing the last two little chicks. He did not understand that I was the protector and defender of his flock and probably his best friend.

You can imagine the turmoil it created when I went running to the house, screaming with pain and shock, blood running down my face and onto my shirt. My mother and sister ran quickly to administer first aid and then called my father from the field. As with any head wound, there was a lot of blood, so it appeared a lot worse than it really was. That being said, I still bear the scar on my upper lip fifty-six years later. As a result of that episode people have gifted me with a collection of ceramic hens and roosters numbering into the thirties which decorate the top of my kitchen cupboard and serve to remind me of that day.

After we arrived back home from the hospital, my father was bound and determined to have revenge on that rooster. We all tried, without success, to dissuade him from carrying out the massacre of the king, but in the end, the rooster died of a heart attack while Dad was trying to capture him. Now *that* was a real tragedy!

A Hen's Dismay

The spring after the demise of King Rooster, we got a new white rooster, a White Rock we called Rocky. He was much more docile, so the hen yard was a safer place for a girl of seven. Those chickens were excellent layers, so Mom and I had enough eggs for our family's use as well as some to trade at the general store for sugar and tea or treats for me. This was in the days before government regulations prevented people who owned small farms from trading eggs, chickens, or produce for things they could not raise themselves. Besides the eggs, we also sold cream to the local dairy, and the cream Cheque was the only bit of income we had until the harvest was completed in the fall. The eggs that spring and summer allowed us some luxuries, such as real soap rather than the homemade lye soap, Blue Ribbon tea, and real vanilla extract.

About April, we found three chickens that had decided to hatch their eggs by setting on a small number of eggs. This instinct often causes a chicken to find what she thinks is a safe place where she will lay a clutch of up to ten eggs and then set upon them, keeping them warm until they hatch. If the farmer does not find her, this could be disastrous, as predators may find her or a cat or dog could steal her eggs if they are looking for a treat. When we found such a hen, we would take her to a safe place, usually a small empty grain bin, where she could set safely in a big box of straw, and we could provide her with food and water.

Another way to tell if a chicken wants to set is by a change in her voice, which becomes a deeper clucking sound; hence the term *cluck* for a chicken that wants to hatch eggs. This whole process is similar to pregnancy in humans. My mother saw it as a bonus because she could have fifteen to twenty chicks per hatch without having to buy them.

By the time the fourth chicken began to cluck, we didn't have enough eggs to set her, and Dad was ready to lock her away until she overcame the instinct to set. But that evening, we visited a neighbor over the hill who gave Mom a good idea; well, it seemed like a good idea at the time. When Mom told her about all the clucks we had set, Mrs. Siebert told her she had a bunch of fresh duck eggs from her flock of ducks that should hatch just fine using the chicken to incubate them instead of a mother duck. Mom had never tried or even thought to try this before, so home we went with fifteen beautiful, aqua duck eggs.

The cluck accepted them without question and took to incubating them as if they were her own with care, turning them regularly. I would often visit her, sitting in the corner of the small grain bin she was in, talking to her quietly because I thought she was lonely. I became quite attached to her, and she grew used to my visits so that she didn't even leave her nest when I came with her food and water.

One day about two weeks into incubation time, we heard her making a really loud racket. When Mom and I went to see what her problem was, we found a newly hatched duckling sitting among the rest of the eggs in her nest. He had hatched well in advance of his siblings for some reason, and the hen knew by instinct she could not continue incubating the other eggs as well as care for the new baby. Usually all the eggs in a clutch hatch together, and the only thing that could have happened was that this egg had started incubation under the mother duck. Perhaps we should have taken this as a warning about what was still to come!

We had to take Donald, as I promptly named him, into the house to reside in a box in the warm space behind the kitchen stove and took to mothering him with all my heart. I cuddled him under my t-shirt when he got cold, and the two of us could be found together from then on. I still remember the feel of his soft, somewhat slippery fuzz when he would crawl up my belly to poke his head out of the neckline of my shirt where he would settle down for a nap. Because he had never had another mother except me, he became imprinted with me and followed me around the house and yard when I did my chores. He would sit on the front step outside the kitchen door after Mom had banished him from her kitchen for pooping on the floor. There he would quack very loudly until I came out and shared some food with him. I had become Mother Duck and didn't mind one bit.

About a week or so later, the rest of the eggs hatched, and Mama Hen and her little brood of waddlers were released from their home in the grain bin. She came into the hen yard, clucking proudly with the whole flock strung out single file behind her as ducks do. She didn't seem to notice anything strange about her brood, but they definitely set the other hens to cackling. About the third day, there was a real uproar as the hens gathered around their shallow pan of water. Mom sent me running to see what was happening. All fourteen little ducks had climbed up a rock that had been anchoring the pan and were now swimming round and round as happy as can be, while Mama Hen and her hen friends scolded them hysterically.

We all had a good laugh, but the fun didn't end there! Mama Hen tried to teach them to run after and catch grasshoppers, but they waddled and were just too slow. She was totally disconcerted by their inability to scratch and peck, and flew into a total rage when they did not respond to her call to try some tasty morsel. You see, they simply did not speak chicken, and conversely, she did not speak duck. Instead, they shoveled up the chopped grain Dad put out for them and went to graze on new spring wheat at the edge of the field.

I think the worst day for Mama Hen was the day they all escaped her custody and went swimming in the pond next to the calf pasture. She ran frantically back and forth along the shore, flapping her wings, and clucking her best, "Come out of there, you foolish children!" until she was totally exhausted. We understood her frustration and felt sorry for her, but we were not surprised when she finally gave up after a couple of days and came back to the hen yard, defeated. The other hens seemed to shun her after that for being a poor mother, and she never laid eggs again after that.

I finally had to give my pet duck his freedom, so I led Donald down to join his brothers and sisters at the pond on the day that Dad made a safe little house and fence that reached out into the water. He was head and shoulders taller than the rest, so he naturally took the position of ringleader as they swam or grazed.

My mother chalked up that adventure to experience, and we never tried anything like that again. I still laugh when I remember that poor hen trying to get her babies out of the pond. This story has entertained a lot of people, as I have told it over and over at special dinners when duck is on the menu. So ends the comedy!

As I wrote these stories, I remembered Noah, and I admit to wondering what stories he must have had to tell after being penned up in the ark with so many animals for so long. A friend, knowing that I was writing this story, brought me a comic illustration of Noah reaching over the side of the ark with a butterfly net, trying to capture a woodpecker who was drilling holes on the outside of the ship. That reminded me of the woodpecker story, "A Wake-Up Call" also in this book.

The Bible tells us that Noah was chosen to save the animals and mankind because he walked with God. Scholars tell us it probably took him about a hundred years to build the ship and people thought he was demented for building it so far from water. Despite being ridiculed, Noah followed God's instructions, giving the sinners plenty of time to repent of their sins and avert God's vengeance, which came on them in the form of the great flood.

I once heard a sermon in which the pastor presented these ideas. Using the measurements given in the

Bible researchers have determined that the ark would have had the space of 522 box cars, which would have held 45,000 animals. But since many of the animals that were alive in biblical times are now extinct, today we would only need 188 boxcars to hold the 17,600 species known to man.

Versions of the story of the great flood can be found in the folklore of many nations around the world, and scientists have found evidence of it in the sandstone and rocks around the world as well. The other thing that interests me is that during the recent genome project that studied the genetics of the world, it was discovered that all of mankind can be divided into three main genetic families that can be traced back to three sources.

I leave you with this quote from Genesis where the story of Noah can be found.

Chapter 8:15 quotes God's instructions to Noah;

> Then God said to Noah, "Come out of the ark, you and your wife and your sons and their wives. Bring out every kind of creature that is with you—the birds, the animals, and all creatures that move along the ground—so they can multiply on the earth and be fruitful and increase in number upon it."
>
> And Genesis 9: 1 Then God blessed Noah and his three sons saying to them, "Be fruitful and increase in number and fill the earth."

It is thought that by the time Noah died at the formidable age of 950, a conservative estimate of the generations of his three son's offspring would have been 120,000 souls.

How I Came to Like Beer

I stopped to have a drink after working in the yard on a hot day in August and found a tall, cold, thirst-quenching bottle of beer in the fridge. I don't drink alcoholic beverages as a matter of course, but I must admit I do like a beer on a hot day. As I sat thinking about why I like the taste of beer, my memory wandered back to the first time I tasted it.

When I was somewhere between the ages of six and eight, for the first time, my father allowed me to ride along in the big truck when he hauled wheat to the grain elevators in town. He did this in order to answer my questions about what happened to the wheat when he took it to town.

That first time my father allowed me to come with him was one of the times that I felt really connected to my father. He was a rather quiet man who was usually busy with the livestock and farming chores. The work of running a farm kept him outside and occupied with machines and animals that were too dangerous for a little girl to be around. Up until that day when I was allowed to go to town with him, if I had asked to accompany him to the field or to the barn, he would just say, "No!" adding that he did not have the time to watch me and keep me from getting in "harms way." Until I was older, I thought that "harm's way" was another person who lived in the barn and who helped my father with his work. But I digress.

On that hot day in late summer, when I saw him getting ready to go to town, my child's brain clicked into gear, seeing a trip to town as a means of escape from the boredom of shelling peas with my sisters and an avenue into the mysterious world of my father. I had to promise that I would stay in the truck unless he allowed me to get out and to not whine or cry. So I dutifully washed my face and changed my clothing and climbed up onto the big bench seat in the 1952 blue Fargo truck for the seven-mile ride to Golden Prairie, Sask. and the closest grain elevators.

The trip was pleasant, but Dad told me I had too much to say after the first couple of miles. I didn't know what that meant, but Dad reinforced it with the statement, "Silence is golden," which I understood very well because he said it often when he was trying to listen to the radio. So I found another way to amuse myself by counting fence posts as they slipped by mile after mile. Soon we reached town and the elevator yard.

There was a lineup of other trucks loaded with the red-gold of prairie grain—number one northern, the best flour-making wheat in the world, we learned later that year in class, that was shipped to every country in the world. In those days, the Great Plain of Saskatchewan was known as the "Breadbasket of the World," as we grew more wheat than any other country in the world except the Russian Steppes. When the Russians had a crop failure a few years later, they bought our wheat to replace their flour supply.

So we waited in the hot, dusty, old truck for our turn to be weighed and to have our sample graded before we could dump our load and have our permit book stamped. Dad took the time to walk me around the elevator to show me where the grain went down into the pit and then was lifted into the huge storage bin until the next rail day when boxcars would be loaded with the beautiful grain from all the farms in the area and hauled to the huge storage facility at Thunder Bay. From there, it would be loaded into large seagoing ships that would take it through the Great Lakes and the Saint Laurence Seaway out across the Atlantic Ocean to other lands. It was an exciting time to be growing up, as we were on the cusp of what today is called globalization. In those years, the markets and people on every continent were clamoring for more of what the Canadian farmers could produce.

From then on, I accompanied Dad to town as often as he would let me, and I think he enjoyed my company during the long wait before he could unload. Depending on how long we had to wait, we would walk the three blocks to downtown to buy groceries and get the mail. Then we would read the funny papers or letters from my older sisters who had already left home to work in the city.

On a particularly hot day near the end of August, when the line of trucks wound down the driveway from the elevator out onto the street, Dad suggested we take a walk to visit an old friend, Ole Madsen. Ole was one of a strange breed of men who had come to our community from Norway. These were men who had come without families to find work, and after making some money working for the Canadian Pacific Railway or some other enterprise, they invested in farmland in the community surrounding Golden Prairie. They had remained bachelors and mainly kept to themselves.

But Ole was one who had broken free of his hermit life and had become an integral part of the community. He was a strong voice for education and sat on the town council. He volunteered at baseball games and loved the children, even though he was shunned by most because he seldom bathed or washed his clothing. His mode of transportation was an old bike, much repaired, which he rode downtown to get his mail and groceries and to visit friends short distances out in the country. He rode that bike almost to the day he was moved by a unanimous community decision to the old folk's home in Maple Creek at age ninety-two. He was a noted horticulturalist, very well read, and respected for his knowledge about plants and world affairs. Men would consult with him about political decisions, plant or animal diseases, and infestations of pests. Women came for advice about gardening as he was a real source of knowledge. He came to every sports day at school and the baseball tournament every July first, where he handed out quarters to every student. A quarter bought a hot dog and pop or a Dixie cup of ice cream in those days. He would turn up at church for the holiday services, especially if the children were giving a performance or there was a church supper after the service.

He was in his late seventies by the time I met him and had retired from farming some years before to live in town, one block from the Baptist church and right across the street from the grain elevators in a CPR skid shack that had provided shelter for the men working on the rail line. Now it was Ole's permanent residence.

Old Ole's Place, as it was commonly called, consisted of one room that had a coal and woodstove that was his only source of heat and used for cooking. There was an old cupboard on the west wall, a small table and a couple of rickety, old chairs that had once been painted blue along the east wall, and a sagging cot that neatly fit at the north end of the shack. Every surface was stacked with reading material: newspapers from other countries, magazines, such as *The Western Producer* and *National Geographic*, and western novels, which he loved.

Outside the shack, his front yard was filled with every variety of vegetable and flower that would grow in our harsh prairie climate and some you would not expect to find. He grew all of his own vegetables and always shared his bounty with others. His peonies and roses were the envy of every woman who planted a flower garden. At the back of the lot sat an old Model T, which he had driven for years but now sat propped up on cement blocks. Most days, when he wasn't working in his yard or out riding around town on his bike, you could find Old Ole sitting in the front seat of the car with a magazine or book resting on the steering wheel while he read. Every inch of the car, including the backseat and trunk, was filled to capacity with magazines he had read but were just too precious to part with.

Reading James 3: especially verses13 and 17 while I paused from my gardening caused me to think of this fine old man who was mentor and friend to all he knew.

"Who is wise and understanding among you? Let him show it by his good life, by deeds done in the humility that comes from wisdom."

"The wisdom that comes from heaven is first of all pure; then peace loving, considerate, submissive, full of mercy and good fruit, impartial, and sincere.

Peacemakers who sow in peace raise a harvest of righteousness."

Dad had become friendly with Ole over the years and admitted to admiring the man his simple lifestyle, generosity, and the amazing amount of knowledge he had accumulated through reading. Dad brought him home on several occasions, and they enjoyed the time they spent together, looking after the cattle and walking through the fields of golden grain. Ole was really shy around women but loved to come for dinner. Mom would make his favourite meal of creamed young chicken with homemade dill pickles, new potatoes, corn on the cob, and freshly baked bread with butter. Mother was famous for her bread and buns, and I remember Ole holding a slice of her freshly baked bread up to the light to admire the fine texture and evenly spaced bubbles that she had achieved in the kneading process.

On that hot day in August, Dad and I found Old Ole sitting on the front step of his skid shack with an old shoe in one hand and a jar of his own golden honey in the other. After their initial greeting, Dad inquired what he was doing.

"I'm killin' ants!" he answered.

"Why?" we wanted to know.

"Little guys get too big for their britches!" he answered. "The colony gets too big, and they come looking for food in my cupboard. So I'm showin' 'em whose boss in this yard."

He poured a little more honey on the sidewalk. We waited until six or seven ants had collected at the little pool of sweet whereupon Ole whacked them with the heel of the old shoe.

With some satisfaction, he placed the shoe near the entrance to their underground home and slowly stood.

"There. Now the workers will go back and tell the rest not to come this way. They're smart, you know! If humans were half as smart as ants, no tellin' what we could achieve. But you didn't come to hear about ants. I saw that long lineup over there and thought I might have a visitor or two. Come on in out of this blazin' sun!"

We followed Ole into his lair. It was the first time I had been inside. I was very curious but dismayed when I saw the dirt on the floor and the general disarray of the place, which was such a contrast to my mother's sparkling, white kitchen. He went around clearing the chairs and tabletops of reading material, all the while talking to Dad about the state of the harvest. I was totally intimidated and stood pressed against Dad's side. Ole took note of this and pulled another stool from under the table, which he made a great show of dusting off with his grimy tea towel.

"There you go, princess!" he said. "Have a seat. Would you like a cup of coffee? I was about to make some for myself."

He reached into the coal pail that resided beside the stove and retrieved some "cow chips" to feed the smoldering coals in the belly of the old stove. Dad declined the offer when he saw Ole reach into the coffee can with the same hand he had just handled the cow dung without taking the time to wash. "It's a little hot for coffee," Dad politely refused.

"I know just the thing." Ole pried up a loose board in the floor of the shack, reached into the resulting hole, and pulled out a couple of tall, cool Lethbridge pilsners. "My fridge," he nodded at the hole in the floor, laughing. "Now what are we goin' to give the princess?" Without consulting Dad, he took a chipped, blue cup from

the cupboard, poured two fingers of the fizzing, yellow brew, and set it in front of me.

"She's too young!" Dad protested.

"Oh, George, loosen up. She's . . . what . . . at least seven! It'll do her good . . . give her an appetite! Maybe put some meat back on her bones!" Ole pinched my very thin arm. I had had yellow jaundice the year before, and Ole had been consulted about how to help me recover from the long illness.

That was my first taste of beer. Today I remember the slightly sour taste of that cool, effervescing brew that quenched my thirst on that hot August afternoon as if it were yesterday.

Although I don't have one often, I have liked the taste of beer ever since. But more than that, the taste of beer transports me back to that little prairie town when life was simpler and friendships were important, to a time when we lived off the land and shared what we had, to a place and time where everyone had value and was cared for and respected by the community. Indeed, where we *were* community!

Thanks for the memories and your good example Old Ole! Here's one for you!

Serious Business

After homesteads were established on the prairies, one-room schoolhouses were built so that the children of the farm families could be educated. These tiny, clapboard buildings became the hub for the entire community, used not only as a school but also as a place to hold meetings and celebrations. Grades one to eight were taught by just one teacher, who also had the responsibility to clean the school, heat it in winter, maintain discipline, and make sure there was a Christmas concert and commencement exercises. The teacher was either housed in a separate 'teacherage' or was billeted with a local family.

Our school, a tiny, white building with black trim, stood a half-mile south of our house and was called Victory Hill. Many of the small schools were given military-sounding names in recognition of the returning soldiers and the victories of World War I. The teacher might be a young man or woman, usually single, fresh out of normal school, which was all the training one needed to become a teacher in those years. My brothers and sisters attended classes in that school, and the teacher lived with our family. One or two of those teachers, whom Mom and Dad "adopted," became so close to our family that they continued to keep in touch with my parents until both Mom and Dad passed away.

Finally, the population grew, and a school board was formed. Inspectors were then hired to ensure that the teacher and students were making progress. I believe the decision to close the little schools and centralize education in one larger school was because the curriculum and standards differed widely from school to school.

For a few years, there was no transportation supplied, so farm children had to be billeted in town with relatives or friends. The government paid a small part of the room and board, but soon buses were supplied to bring the children to and from school so that they could remain at home with their parents.

When I began school in 1956, I rode with my older sister Mildred on a brand-new school bus driven by Mr. Jaster. We lived only seven miles from town, but because we were the farthest away, we had to get on first, which meant we rode about thirty miles before we had picked up all the other children and reached the school. Mr. Jaster was a serious and well-organized man. He and his wife, Julia, lived on the edge of town, about a block from the Baptist church, where both of them were recognized as fine, upstanding members of the congregation. Mrs. Jaster played the piano for church services, and Mr. Jaster was a deacon. Mrs. Jaster taught piano lessons to the young people who wished to learn, and Mr. Jaster farmed and helped to build roads, etc., as needed. Since Mr. Jaster was respected in the community, when the need arose for trustworthy men to drive school buses, he was one of the first hired.

Driving a school bus was serious business, as you were literally responsible for the lives of the children while they were in your care. Most of the drivers had their work cut out for them because the roads were terrible in those years, little more than prairie trails that deteriorated to the status of mud bog every time it rained or during spring thaw. During the winter, they were often blocked by huge snowdrifts that required a very skillful driver to push through safely. The driver often seemed to force that little bus, which was little more than a tin can on wheels, through huge drifts by sheer force of will. He would survey the depth and consistency of the snow, and then he would issue the order, "Hang on, kids!" Backing up, he would take a run at the drift. If we didn't get all the way through the first time, he would back up again and again until he succeeded, forcing a path through the drift. Many times, we all had to get out to help push or shovel so that we could get to school at all. The children of that era were not pampered or protected, and we often arrived at school disheveled and mud-spattered.

One spring after a particularly snowy winter, there was a quick thaw that resulted in more mud bogs and running water than usual. One farm, where we picked up three children, had a seasonal creek running through the valley a half-mile from their house. It was located about six feet from the main road to town, making it almost impossible to drive through. We would come in from the north following the pasture trail, pick up the three children, turn west and go down the hill at a high rate of speed in order to make it through the creek and then make an immediate left turn onto the main road. There is not a roller coaster in existence that can hold a candle to the excitement of that ride! However, it soon became evident that there was a problem.

The father of the three children had allowed his cattle into the field to graze, which meant that often there were cows on the pathway down the hill. It also meant that the gate through the fence, which ran along the road, had to remain closed to prevent the cows from escaping.

The first morning's episode went like this: We had to stop the bus to chase the cattle off the trail, and then because we had to stop to open the gate, we were not going fast enough when we hit the creek, which resulted in the bus becoming mired running board deep in the middle of the fast-flowing water. The farmer had to then haul us out with his tractor, which made us late for school.

The second morning, the bus driver sent one of the oldest boys to clear the cows from the path and open the gate, which helped us get through the creek successfully. However, even though the boy was wearing high-topped rubber boots, they had filled with water while he waded through the creek, resulting in his having wet feet for the rest of the day. On the third day, that boy had to stay at home because he had caught cold. So the bus driver had a long, serious conversation with the farmer, informing him that from then on he would be responsible for clearing the path of cattle and making sure the gate was open if he wanted his children to be picked up by the school bus! That helped, and we made it through successfully for the rest of the week.

However, by Monday of the next week, the farmer had to go to town early, leaving the bus driver to contend with errant cattle and the closed gate on his own once more. Tuesday was much the same story. By Wednesday, this normally calm man, who drove the bus with such skill and took such good care of us, lost his patience. He stopped at the top of the hill to survey the scene. Then he issued the familiar order, "Hang on, kids!" after which he took off like a charging bull, leaning on the horn all the way. The cows cleared the path with tails up and wide eyes bulging at the sight of this orange torpedo blasting its way through the herd. Hang on we did, as we hit the creek at breakneck speed, continuing on through the water and hitting the  closed gate with such force that we lifted the fence poles out of the ground for a half a mile on either side. The bus made a wild left turn onto the high road, dragging the gate and all the barbed wire underneath and behind it, only coming to a stop a quarter mile down the road when the wire became so firmly wrapped around the axles and undercarriage of the bus that it could no longer move. We came to a screeching stop and piled out to see the damage. It took Mr. Jaster and the older boys at least two hours to cut and untangle the mess under the bus, during which time we children enjoyed a small holiday, reading or playing tag on the road.

The next day, there was a real shouting match over who would be responsible for rebuilding the fence. Finally, the school district agreed to pay for the materials, and Mr. Jaster humbly condescended to help the farmer rebuild it. It was also decided that the farmer's three children must be at the road when the bus arrived from then on so that the rest of the children would not be placed in peril or miss school because of their creek or cows.

Many years later, Mr. Jaster was elected to the town council and was known for his good sense and calm wisdom. On a certain Thursday, he came home for lunch, placing his coat on the back of his chair and his fedora, which he was used to wearing, on top of the sewing machine. Mr. and Mrs. Jaster ate a hearty lunch and rested in the living room for a short time. Then Mr. Jaster rose to ready himself for the town council meeting, which was to take place at two o'clock. He brushed his hair, shrugged into his jacket and, with his hat in hand, kissed his wife, and went out the door. She called after him from the doorway, requesting he pick up the mail. He waved, and she turned to clean up the dishes from lunch and ready herself for the two young girls who would soon come for piano lessons after school. As she wiped the kitchen table, she noticed that something seemed to be missing from the top of the sewing machine, but in her haste, she shrugged it off and continued with her chores.

Meanwhile, Mr. Jaster, having stopped for the mail at the post office, met an old friend who engaged him in a long conversation, causing him to arrive at the town council meeting a little later than he had hoped.

He walked in just in time to hear a proposal to raise property taxes being tabled. "I OBJECT!" he said before he had even found a seat or removed his coat and hat. The entire assembly turned to see who was speaking and, upon seeing him, promptly broke out in such a fit of laughter that all thought of serious discussion was extinguished. Mr. Jaster stood with disbelief, wondering why his objection had garnered this hilarious response. The man nearest to him rose and, doffing the fedora from Mr. Jaster's head, asked, "Is this the latest fashion?"

Sticking out from under the brim of his fedora, dear old Mr. Jaster saw the nicely starched, white frill of his wife's hand-crocheted doily. He grabbed the hat out of the man's hand, peeled the doily off the felt brim, and stuffed it into his pocket without ceremony, wondering why his friend at the post office had not warned him of the oddity. He sat down red-faced, the wind gone completely out of the lusty intentions with which he had entered the room.

Mrs. Jaster was happy to get her doily back as it was a particularly intricate pattern, but the members of the council never let Mr. Jaster forget the incident. Much to his chagrin, they often lifted the hat from his head when they met on the street to see if he had anything under it.

These days, when I see the school buses arriving at our local school and hear the bus drivers complaining about the weather, I'm reminded of that little orange bus and Mr. Jaster and am transported down the corridors of time to that simpler time and place of my youth.

The Jasters took their responsibilities in the church and community seriously. They were people of integrity. I found these verses from Psalm 7: 6b-8 that make me think of them: "Awake, My God; decree justice. Let the assembled peoples gather around you. Rule over them from on high; let the Lord judge the peoples. Judge me, O Lord, according to my righteousness, according to my integrity, O Most High."

An Easter Surprise

I was driving down a country road the other day when I came to a picturesque farm where a small herd of sheep was grazing in a field beside the road. The sight of them reminded me of my Uncle August, who kept a small herd of sheep among the menagerie of animals on his farm. A neighbor had given him a couple of lambs one spring, and after a few years, he had a flock of about thirty adult ewes that produced a fine flock of lambs each year.

They were particularly well suited to grazing on the type of land that Uncle August owned, as it was the arid pasture of southern Saskatchewan where a short type of grass called prairie wool grew. The sheep became an important part of the farm, both for food and income. My uncle sheared the sheep every spring, and the fleece was shipped to a woolen mill to be made into blankets and spun into yarn used to make clothing. The sheep were happy to get rid of their heavy winter coats in the spring, and Uncle August was happy to receive a nice Cheque from the woolen mill.

When I was ten, lambing time came sometime in March, and I begged to visit Uncle's farm to see the new lambs. So on a lovely, warm Sunday afternoon in early April, we drove the eighteen miles from our farm to his. While the adults visited, my cousins and I ran wild and free past the animals in the barnyard to the hills where the sheep grazed and the lambs frolicked as if they had springs in their legs.

Later in the day, we got to feed the lambs that were penned at the bottom of the garden, which I found out were either orphaned or the second born of a set of twins. When a ewe has twins, she somehow understands when she does not have enough milk to feed two, so she will reject the smallest one in order to save the other. In the wild, this is called "selection of the fittest," and the instinct to continue this process is strong even today among domesticated sheep.

Well, on Uncle's farm, the little ones who were rejected by Mama were fed cow's milk using a long-necked bottle with a large rubber nipple. I got to feed one of the orphans, and much to my delight, the lamb knelt in the soft hay and began sucking vigorously. I had to hang onto the bottle with both hands to keep it from being pulled out of my hands. His little bum was up, and his tail, which had not yet been docked, was waggling at great speed, showing his appreciation for the warm milk.

Of course, I fell in love with the little creature and begged to take him home as a pet. The adults explained that lambs did not stay little for long, and that they needed a lot of care as they grew, but it was all to no avail. I had fallen in love and could not be dissuaded from my desire. Sadly, I was not allowed to take a lamb home that day and cried myself to sleep that night.

About two weeks later, we attended the Easter service at the local church. My uncle and aunt rarely attended because they lived about thirty miles from the church, a long distance to travel in those days, so this was a really special day for my cousins and me. I remember the message we heard that Sunday was about how Jesus is called the Lamb of God. We heard how the Hebrews used sheep as a sacrifice to atone for their sins, so Jesus became the sacrificial lamb when he died for the sins of the world on the cross. We learned that sheep were a common commodity in the Middle East at that time, so people could relate to the comparisons made between their behaviour and that of sheep when they went astray.

After the service ended, my cousin dragged me away from my friends toward their truck. All of our friends followed and gathered around while my uncle lifted a very large cardboard box from the back of their truck. My cousin urged me to look inside, and what do you think I found there? Lying on a bed of hay was the sweetest little lamb I had ever seen! He was so small, only two days old, and my cousin had tied a blue ribbon around his neck to show that he was a boy. My uncle told me that he was mine if I wanted him. I ran to ask Mom and Dad and, to my delight, they said yes, as long as I would be responsible for his care and feeding. I was in heaven as only a ten year old could be and promptly named him Lambkin. This was the beginning of a loving relationship that lasted nearly three years.

At first, I was so excited that I would run down to the barn while I was still in my pajamas to see my new friend. He learned his name quickly and came to me when I called him, especially if I had a bottle, which reminded me of that Jesus had said, "My sheep know my voice." I bottle-fed Lambkin until he was old enough to drink milk from a pail and eat chopped grain from a dish in his pen.

That whole first summer, he followed me around the barnyard like a puppy and loved the treats of tender green shoots of grain I brought for him. He was still small enough so I could pick him up and hold him while he slept. I could tell that he was growing because he was getting heavier and his wool grew thick and curly as summer came. He loved to lie in the shade under the trees that grew near the pond during the heat of the day, and I often joined him there, reading out loud to him as if he could understand.

I spent a lot of time in and around the barn that year and learned a lot about taking care of animals. I learned what it meant to be a good shepherd—keeping him clean, well fed, and safe from coyotes. However, my lovely summer routine with Lambkin changed when I had to go back to school in the fall. I had to leave early on the school bus so I didn't have as much time to spend with him, but he still loved to follow me when I came into the barnyard in the evenings after I had finished my homework and on Saturdays. He soon grew too big to hold and became more independent, learning to follow the cows to the pasture where he grazed all day.

After Lambkin's second birthday, Dad said that since he was no longer my little playmate and was now a beautiful two-year-old ram, he should be sold. He had also become a bit of a pest because although we had weaned him off milk from a pail when he was about six months old, Lambkin still loved milk and would drink a whole pail full if you left it sitting where he could get into it. It was so funny watching my brother trying to drag Lambkin away from the fresh milk that had just come from milking the cow. What was even funnier was watching Lambkin after he succeeded in getting his head into a full pail of milk. He would come up for air, blowing milky bubbles with his face and ears coated in froth while his fat, little belly grew even fatter as he trotted away, giving a satisfied little *baa*.

He had become a nuisance because he had also learned to wiggle through the fence in order to get to the lovely vegetables in Mom's garden. He looked so funny with lettuce leaves or carrots dangling from his mouth while he happily munched. That made Mom really angry, and she would chase him with a broom until he went back to the barnyard. She also wanted to sell my precious lamb, but I loved him and could not bear to be parted from him. So I begged and cajoled my parents until they agreed to keep him for one more summer.

That loving relationship came to an abrupt end near fall because my brother Ernie had taught him to fight. He began pushing Lambkin around by grabbing his newly developed horns or teasing him like a bullfighter by waving a rag or sack until Lambkin chased him. Lambkin loved this new form of play, which appealed to his new male instincts, and it was great fun watching him use those budding horns as he bunted hay bales and rolled pails around the barnyard, spilling the contents.

One day, my mother, who often helped my dad with chores in the barnyard, came to help move a large water trough. Mom wore one of Dad's old red-checked farm shirts, and it fluttered in the breeze when she bent over the trough with a small pail to bail out the water. Lambkin must have thought she was teasing him like my brother often did. He watched her for a while, bleating loudly as if to give her a warning. Then he lowered his big, wooly head with the curly little horns and aimed at my mother's ample backside. Lambkin had grown really big that spring and summer and could move really fast. Before my dad could shout a warning, Lambkin achieved his goal with a solid thump. He hit Mom squarely in the left hip, lifting her up and over the end of the trough where she landed with a plop in the mud. Thankfully, she wasn't injured too badly. The bruises on her hip soon healed, but her wounded pride was another matter, which soon turned into anger directed at my brother and me for teaching Lambkin to fight and bunt. Needless to say, Lambkin's days on the farm were numbered after that episode. My dad declared there would be no further argument; Lambkin would be sold at the next Tompkins sheep sale.

My beautiful pet did achieve his hour of fame and glory at the sale as he was given an award for "Best Ram at Show" and fetched a more handsome price than any of us expected. A man who owned a large sheep ranch in the south end of The province bought him and assured me that Lambkin would have a good home. Dad explained to me that he would be the father of his own flock and would have many little Lambkins. I guess all that special care and feeding helped him to grow and develop into an extra fine male specimen.

We used the money from the sale of Lambkin to buy new winter coats for the family, and Mom said she felt she had been reimbursed for the pain and embarrassment he had caused her as she snuggled into the stylish woolen coat that kept her warm when the cold winter winds blew.

Did you know that sheep are mentioned 189 times in Scripture and were a main source of food and clothing in the Middle East in biblical times? One of the most famous Scriptures using the example of sheep with a shepherd is Psalm 23: 1and 2 "The LORD is my Shepherd. I shall not want. He makes me lie down in green pastures; He leads me beside the still waters." When Lambkin came into my life, I didn't know much about caring for sheep, but I soon learned that they will not drink from a fast-running stream. So the Good Shepherd leads his flock to a place where the water is quiet so they might drink in a place of peace.

In Isaiah 53:6 we are told, "We are like sheep, each going our own way." I often watched my uncle's flock of sheep and found they could get into a great deal of trouble if left to their own devices. Sheep will follow one another blindly into danger. They get hung up in fences and fall over cliffs. We are assured that God's rod and His staff will keep us on the right path much like a shepherd who loves his flock. Jesus, His son will keep us from serious harm in life by watching over us and correcting us as needed. He doesn't use his rod to beat us into submission but as I have experienced He gently catches us with the shepherd's crook before we run headlong into danger.

My Nemesis, The Crow

Today, I read in 1 Kings 17 the story of Elijah, a prophet who lived among the Israelites during the reign of King Ahab. The people had fallen away from God and worshipped idols instead, so He sent Elijah to warn them to stop their wicked ways and return to the worship of the one true God. However, they did not listen to the prophet and continued their idolatrous practices. Finally, God sent a drought to punish these wayward people and to demonstrate His power.

During the drought, God told Elijah to go to the brook in Cherith, which God said would not dry up, where Elijah could drink while the kingdom of Israel suffered a great famine because of their sin. The Lord said to him in 1 Kings 17:4, "You will drink from the brook, and I will have the ravens feed you there."

This summer, I watched a TV documentary made by scientists from the West Coast who had watched and studied the behaviour of a group of crows. What they learned was that crows are almost as smart as humans. They teach their young in much the same way that humans do and even have the ability to recognize human faces. That set me to thinking about how smart crows and ravens are and caused me to remember the following episode from my own life.

When I was about five, my brother Ernie, who was about nineteen at the time, found a fledgling crow that had fallen from its nest, or at least that is what he thought had happened. It was a very curious little bird, so when my brother offered it a piece of his sandwich, it hopped right over to gobble the tasty morsel from his fingers. Before long, the baby crow became a captive and allowed Ernie to pick it up and bring it home. Ernie called him simply Crow because at first none of us knew its gender, and it soon became the family pet, eating from our hands. On second thought, perhaps the term *pet* was a little too innocent; *pest* would have been more accurate.

As soon as Crow had grown a full set of wing feathers, Ernie took the young bird up the ladder that went to the attic on the outside of the house and released it from there in order to teach him to fly. After several attempts, Crow finally found his wings and soared across the yard to the roof of my dad's blacksmith shop. From then on, although he could have flown away to join his wild brothers, Crow never tried. As often as not, you could find him following my brother around the yard, walking behind him as if he were a dog on a leash. He only took flight when he felt it necessary to reach something or to escape from danger.

Danger came in various forms. My mother's broom was one such threat because she could wield it with the dexterity of an athlete at any animal that tried to invade her kitchen. My father also would have loved to catch and do some harm to that crow, especially after he caught the bird stealing his screws, small tools, and machine parts. In fact, the scallywag became the pirate of the farmyard, stealing anything shiny and, making off with these things to his favourite roosting spot, the top shelf in my dad's shop. There, we would find a collection of his treasures, such as Dad's lost  screws, silver gum wrappers, coins, beautiful pebbles, and a spoon someone had forgotten outside on the picnic table. There was even a watch, the owner of which we never did find, and several small tools, which were his favourite things to pilfer. Crow seemed to understand that stealing these things would aggravate the person who had lost them and soon developed the dexterity of the craftiest pickpocket. After the first time we discovered Crow's treasure trove, we knew exactly where to look for articles that suddenly went missing, especially if they were shiny.

Crow became Ernie's nemesis the day he stole the car keys. Ernie had cleaned out the car in anticipation of a date with some friends and made the mistake of leaving the keys in the ignition with the window open. When he came out to leave for town, the keys were gone. He searched in his pockets and the house, and finally he remembered leaving them in the car before he had gone into the house to change clothes. We found the keys in Dad's shop, guarded by Crow himself. My mother said it served Ernie right for leaving the keys in the car and because he was the one who had brought Crow home.

Crow also became my nemesis that summer, as he was not above dragging my dolls out of the doll buggy, tattling to Mom with his loud *caw, caw* when I was about to steal green peas from her garden, or swooping down to steal my snack of toast and jam right out of my fingers when I brought it outside. I remember being both shocked and frightened when he stole my food the first time, his large, black wings whistling near my ears and hitting my head and back as he flew away with my snack. I have never quite gotten over my fear of large birds.

Crow became a real pest toward the end of summer. He learned to swoop down for a ride on Lady's back, the quiet, old draft horse my dad used to till between the rows of potatoes we grew for the hospital and the massive vegetable garden. The first couple of times Crow hitched a ride, Dad had to fight to keep control of Lady, who, dragging my poor father at breakneck speed, was ready to bolt across the field and through the fence in order to escape the screeching demon on her back. However, she was such a placid old soul that she soon learned to tolerate the crow riding high and mighty on her collar, *caw-cawing* instructions for man and beast all the way, as the horse plodded patiently between the rows.

Crow also liked to ride the dog. After the first few whirling bouts, during which feathers flew and snarls and screeches were exchanged, they seemed to come to some sort of an agreement. We could often see dear old Collie, the best dog in the world, allowing the crow to ride on him across the yard when Mom called, "Dinner!" To our surprise, Collie also allowed Crow to peck small morsels from his dish.

Another episode found Crow at odds with the female cat that stalked the bird, never realizing that her dreams of eating Crow were a little too grandiose. She gave it her best try, sneaking through the tall grass and springing out at him while he was eating. After that, Crow loved to torment her. He would fly along just above her and high enough so he could swoop down occasionally to peck at her ears. Then the dear, old tabby would rear up on her hind legs with a ferocious snarl and swipe at him with her long, sharp claws. Of course, she could never catch him, and he would fly off with a call that sounded like laughter.

Crow developed another favourite pastime to torment the poor old cat. Walking behind her, he would peck at the white tip on her twitching tail. Normally such a regal appendage, the cat soon began walking with her tail tucked well beneath her legs and her ears flattened to her head, yowling and growling at the bird as she went.

We called Crow "Bad Boy" so often that he started repeating the words, especially when he saw my mom come out of the house to do chores. He would perch on the ladder to the attic or on the roof of the henhouse when she was gathering eggs and screech, "Bad Boy, Bad Boy" until Mom threatened to get the shotgun.

My father always wore a blue-and-white striped engineer's hat in summer, but that summer he lost several to the lofty treetop. If Dad was greasing the machinery or fixing something that required him to be down on the ground, Crow took the opportunity to sneak up close and, while Dad's hands were occupied, snatch Dad's cap right off his head and quickly fly off with it. I think he learned to do this by watching Dad's nightly game of tag that he played with the dog, using the cap as prize. The only difference was that the dog always brought the cap back, and Crow had a trophy tree decorated with several new blue-and-white hats, the latest spoils of his thieving adventures.

Crow's natural instinct was to tease, and he loved tormenting anything or anyone he could get a rise out of, be they man or animal, friend or foe. He also seemed to sense my mother's dislike for the travelling salesmen who were sometimes a waste of her valuable time. Two of the men my mother hated to see come into our yard more than anyone were the Fuller Brush man, Tom Dwery, and the cattle buyer, Mr. Cornblum.

The Fuller Brush salesman would never take no for an answer. Once he started his sales pitch, he was like a broken record you could not shut off. My mother was too polite to interrupt him and say no, so she usually ended up buying some small thing from him just to get him to leave. He wasted time with his endless sales pitch and bored us to tears with his demonstrations of brushes and other paraphernalia that Mom had neither the money nor the inclination to buy. Mom's policy was to never allow a salesman into the house if Dad was not at home, so she would not open the door for the poor man. One day, as he tried to entice Mom to buy something from outside the door, with his cases full of brushes spread around him on the step, Crow suddenly swooped down, screeching his objections. "Bad boy!" he declared, stealing a brush. That left the poor man no recourse but to beat a hasty retreat to his car, cases and brushes tumbling into the backseat. Because he could not display his wares and had no hope of making a sale, he soon left with Crow screeching along behind him all the way to the gate.

Mr. Cornblum, on the other hand, always smoked a cigar, even in Mom's precious kitchen, while haggling over the price of the latest batch of spring calves. And Mom didn't allow *anyone* to smoke in her kitchen! She grew to appreciate Crow a little more the day he would not allow the big man out of his car. Crow landed on the roof of the black sedan and leaned over the edge to give the salesman the evil eye and a loud screech every time he reached for the door handle. Dad finally came from the barn to investigate and rescued him.

In true salesman character, Mr. Cornblum was loud and aggressive, always swaggering a little when he came to view the calves Dad might have for sale. His trademark stogie that reeked to high heaven and white Fedora hat did not impress Mom one bit. He often made the mistake of coming to call on a Sunday morning about the time Mom and Dad were getting ready for church. Dad would come out of the house, remnants of shaving cream still on his face, and warn this aggressive man that he did not discuss business on Sunday!

It was on one such occasion that Mr. Cornblum met Crow again. We don't know if it was the sound of aggravation in Dad's voice or the smell of smoke rising toward Crow's perch that inspired him to swoop down, cawing loudly, snatch the still-smoking cigar out of the startled man's hand, and flap away, knocking that precious white hat off his head in the process. Before he could protest, Crow flew off, higher and higher, finally dropping the stinking thing like a bomb to its perdition on the road. Mother gave Crow a special treat of jam toast that day after Mr. Cornblum left, a much humbler man. After that, he always left his hat and cigar in the car when he came to call.

Some of Crow's antics were invented out of pure boredom. Not having friends of his own species inspired him to invent other ways to amuse himself. He learned to repeat sounds he heard often. He could screech like the rusty hinge on the calf pasture gate and could imitate other birds, including our old rooster. He could *putt putt* like the neighbor's John Deere tractor and say several words such as *bad boy* and *pretty girl*, which he followed with a long, low whistle, a taunt I'm sure my brother had taught him.

As he matured, Crow became more restless and his pranks became more obnoxious. My mother became less tolerant of him because he hung around the kitchen door most of the time, stealing food from the other animals and from me when I brought my snacks outside. We could no longer have a meal out under the trees, as he would poke his beak into every plate and cup and would eye every dish on the table, trying to steal something when we weren't watching.

Mom finally ran out of patience completely on the morning she laundered the guest room sheets. We did laundry in a Wringer washer in those days, a back-breaking task. First, you had to carry the water from the well, and then you had to heat the water on the stove. Next, you had to fill the machine and add soap, and finally, you were ready to put in the clothing. When the washing was finished, each piece had to go through the wringers. Then it all had to be rinsed in a tub of clean water by hand, and then fed through the wringers again. I tell you this so you will understand just how much time and effort the whole procedure took.

Anyway, Mom was finally hanging the last of the sheets on the line to dry after washing and rinsing them by hand. This was quite a chore as they were large and very heavy to lift up onto the clothesline. She finally put the last clothespin in place with a sigh of relief and turned just in time to see Crow drop the last clothespin from his yellow beak and watch in horror as the corner of the last of the wet sheets went sliding off the line to drop down to the ground with the rest of the wet laundry. Doing a balancing act on the clothesline as easily as any tightrope walker, Crow had left a trail of muddy clothing and clothespins behind him. He eyed her then, tilted his head from side to side as if trying to gauge what her reaction might be to his latest trick, and said a tentative, "Bad boy?"

That was the final straw for Mother. She gathered the muddy sheets and pillowcases back into the basket and stormed into the house, muttering, "Just wait! Just you wait!" She set the soiled laundry aside in the porch, and when my brother came in for lunch, she pounced on him, saying, "This is your fault! You brought that bird home!" Then she laid the law down as she displayed the muddy clothing and sheets. "That crow must go!" Our Mother never shouted, but she did while showing my brother the sheets. "I don't care what you do with him! I just want him gone!" She ended her tirade almost in tears.

That afternoon, Ernie lured Crow into Dad's shop with his favourite food, jam bread, so he could capture him. Then he set off to find a new home for him. He released him about five miles away from the farm where he had first found him as a fledgling, thinking that he would rejoin his own crow family. That was two o'clock. By six o'clock, when we sat down for supper, there was Crow, cawing for his supper on his favourite perch, the gatepost outside the kitchen door.

About a week later, Ernie went to visit friends who lived about twenty miles away, and Crow went along for the ride. We had a blessed three days of peace until he returned swooping down to ride on Lady's collar while Dad was plowing the potato tops into the earth before winter. So we gave up trying to get him to leave and reconciled ourselves to his antics, except for Mother, who guarded her wet sheets on the line with the broom.

As fall came with the trees changing colour and the evenings becoming cooler, the crows in the neighborhood began to do practice flights before the migration south. Crow would sit and watch as they swooped and played in the air currents. They would come, en masse, and sit in the now bare poplar trees, calling loudly to each other as we picked pumpkins, the last of the corn, and squash. Crow cocked his head from side to side, seeming to listen, and sometimes he could not resist joining in their acrobatics in the sky.

One morning, the murder of crows seemed to be larger and noisier than usual, and we watched with interest as we did chores. Crow sat quietly by the kitchen door as we had breakfast. Then he flapped his wings and giving his famous

"Bad Boy" call, flew off to join his feathered family as they did a final swoop and wheel over the yard before heading south to warmer climes. We went about our chores with a sigh of relief, but soon an air of melancholy settled over the yard, for it seemed to be just too quiet.

For the next three summers, Crow came back to visit, sitting on the gatepost and saying, "Bad Boy" in greeting, but he never came back to stay now that he had found friends of his own species. We watched as he helped build a huge nest of twigs in the poplar trees on the edge of our land, and soon he had fledglings of his own to care for. During those three years, I still lost the occasional snack, Mom guarded her clothesline on wash days with the broom close at hand, and once in a while Dad lost a cap to the big nest in the trees. But Ernie was never again tempted to pick up a baby crow that had fallen from its nest.

We didn't often see our mother lose her temper but that day I think she must have read this verse and taken it's meaning literally. "Discipline your son, and he will give you peace; he will bring delight to your soul. But blessed is he who keeps the law" (Proverbs 29:17-18). As Mom mellowed in the later years of her life, she and Ernie would share the memories of that crow and laugh together.

Gumbo Stew

July first was always a day of celebration in my hometown. Aside from celebrating Dominion Day or Canada Day as it is known today, it was also the day chosen by the town to hold The Golden Prairie Annual Sports Day and Baseball Tournament. Three small prairie towns formed a triangle in that southwest corner of Saskatchewan, and there was stiff competition between the sports teams that were organized by their citizens. So July first became a day to visit with friends and relatives who came from miles around, sing *O Canada*, and cheer for the home team.

The day began early with baseball games on all three diamonds in town. The tournament was run as a round robin and, depending on how many teams were entered, would last well into the afternoon. The final game was always held at the official sports ground just west of town. There were also races for the little children, including the potato race, the sack race, and the three-legged race, as well as the one-hundred-yard dash for the older kids. The men from the church served hotdogs and hamburgers, and the ladies served homemade pie by the slice or ice cream Dixie cups with those little wooden spoons.

I had been looking forward to the event for the whole year before I turned ten. You have to understand that baseball was about the most important sport in those little prairie towns. In fact, it was so important that we were even allowed to listen to the World Series in class while studying for June exams. A group of my friends had been discussing how our baseball team was the best and was going to beat the pants off the other teams. Several of us, including myself, had older brothers who were playing on the team, so we formed a cheering section. As the day drew closer, I began to talk more and more about the event, but Mom said she had canning to do because the beans and peas were ready in the garden, and Dad said he had a canvas for the header to repair and couldn't waste the time lolling around town for a whole day of baseball. I begged and cajoled but to no avail. When school was dismissed for the summer after exams the last week of June, I told everyone with a heavy heart that I would not be at the baseball games.

I was always an early riser, and July first dawned hot and clear, the perfect day, I thought, for a ball game. I sulked in my pajamas on the front step, my hand buried in Collie's ruff on the left with the cats cuddled on the other side of me in sympathy. I was feeling very blue indeed when I saw my brother and Mother come from the barn carrying four full pails of milk. Then to my surprise, my brother said, "Well, if you're going to come with me to the sports day, you had better get a wiggle on!" I could hardly believe my ears and looked at Mom, waiting for her to say something.

"We decided you can go with Ernie, but you have to promise to behave. Just mind your Brother, you have to tell him if you want to go with your friends or anything." I didn't even hear the last part, because I jumped up with a hoot, scaring the poor dog and cats from their cozy places, and flew into the house to dress.

I knew exactly what I wanted to wear. My older sisters had given me an early birthday gift during their last visit home from Medicine Hat, a pair of white shorts and a white peasant blouse with a wide lace collar. While Ernie turned the milk separator and Mom did my long, dark hair in French braids, I gobbled down a slice of toast and jam. Mom worked a red ribbon into the braids, tied a big bow at the end of each, and then scrubbed my face until my cheeks were rosy and my nose shone. Ready, I presented myself to my brother who by this time was dressed in his white baseball uniform with the green-and-gold lettering on the back that read, "Golden Prairie Chinooks."

With a final warning from Mom to take care, we were off, literally, to the races. The day was hot and clear, and I was as excited as a kid could be, bouncing up and down on the car seat as we drove off to great adventure.

I found my friends getting organized for the races, so I joined them and ran in as many races as I could. I took second in the sack race, third in the three-legged race I ran with my friend, and we were rewarded with ribbons and suckers for our efforts. We ate hotdogs while sitting in the bleachers while watching the last baseball game and then moved under the seats for protection from the wind, which was the forerunner to the big, dark clouds that had begun to collect on the horizon. Then a friend of my father, an older Norwegian man who we called Old Ole, came to watch the final game and, as was his generous habit, gave each child under twelve a quarter to spend, which in those days bought a pop and a Dixie cup of ice cream. Because of Ole's generosity I had had my fill of sticky, sweet stuff by the time my brother came to pick me up from my place under the bleachers.

We left the grounds as the first fat drops of rain plopped into the dust of the field. The young men shouted, "Congratulations!" and "Better luck next time!" to each other as they ran for cover to the automobiles that were streaming out of the parking lot back toward downtown for hot meals in the café or hotel. We gave my brother's friend Eddy a ride, and I listened to them tell each other how lucky they were to have finished the game before the rain blew in. "Yeh, we almost got to play gumbo ball!" Eddy said and that set them both laughing, but I didn't understand until much later what they were laughing about.

I thought we would go home at that point, but Ernie said that he had been invited to the dance and lunch with his friends, so he had made arrangements for me to stay with Dad's cousin who owned the restaurant. She lived in a small house attached to the restaurant, and her granddaughter, who was my age, was there as well, so we could watch TV together. This was the second great treat of the day because we did not have electricity on the farm nor a TV. Eddy joked, "We're off to the gumbo ball!" as they went off, laughing.

My friend and I watched TV and played throughout the evening until the station signed off for the night. Finally, sometime after midnight after I had fallen asleep on the chesterfield, my brother came to collect me. He wrapped me in a big, woolen blanket and told me it was going to be a tough drive because it had been pouring rain all evening.

At this point, I must digress from the story to explain about gumbo. Now, you may have heard of gumbo, a special type of spicy stew made in Mississippi. But this gumbo is not stew, although it might have the same consistency as stew when wet. According to scientists, this gumbo is naturally occurring clay made up of aluminum silicate deposited during the Ice Age and is more like the Mississippi mud mentioned in the dance song than the yummy stew. The entire countryside around our little town contained large pockets of the stuff. Composed of finely ground minerals mixed with decayed vegetation, it turns into a slimy, sticky mass when wet. If you try to walk any distance in it, your feet get progressively larger and heavier with every step. Driving in it presents an almost impossible challenge, as the mud collects on the tires in much the same way, rendering the heaviest tire tread useless.

That was the challenge my dear brother faced as we began the trip home that fateful night. The rain, driven by the gale force wind, came at us in solid sheet and was so fast that the wipers could hardly keep the window clear. Our 1956 Plymouth, which had been so clean and shiny that morning, was soon covered in mud as the tires fought to keep a grip on the newly graded roadbed.

We had been fighting for a better road for years, as the old one was little better than a prairie trail that had originally been cut by the wagons of the settlers to the area. The old "road" became entirely impassable with the huge drifts that accumulated in the hollows during winter blizzards and again in spring when the melt turned large sections into mud bogs. I had experienced that road firsthand when our school bus fought its way through the mess for the four years since I had turned six. Detouring through people's fields and pastures was frowned upon, so we were all relieved when our appeal for a graded road had finally been granted that spring.

The municipality had hired a crew with an elevator grader, which made a ditch and piled the dirt up on the roadbed at the same time. This process, after it had been graded and packed, made a lovely two-lane road with deep ditches on either side. Well, it was lovely to look at for a little while until someone had to drive on it in the rain. You see, they had created a slightly rounded surface that should have shed the water. However, having stopped just short of real efficiency, they did not gravel the surface, which meant there was little to provide traction. So this night, the first real rainstorm we had had since the road was completed, was the test of its true nature.

From my cozy nest in the back seat, I heard my brother's nasty comments as the car seemed more inclined to leave the rounded surface of the road for the depths of the water-filled ditches. His muttered criticisms of the road crew's abilities were not fit for my tender ears, so I put my hands over my ears and hid in the cocoon of my blanket as we slipped and slid our way home at a snail's pace. He fought the wheel, two feet to the left and corrected back to the right for another two feet, for at least two hours, the length of time it  took us to travel the seven miles from town to our farm. The sweat was dripping from his battle to keep the car on the road when we finally came to a slithering stop in front of the house somewhere just before three o'clock in the morning. We found a welcome light glowing in the window, a little thing Mother insisted on until the last person was safely back home.

Although our parents were angry with my brother for staying at the dance so late and risking the car on the drive home, they soon got over their stewing and were just relieved that we had made it home safely. I think Father even gained new respect for my brother's driving skills that night because he heard that the farmers and their tractors in the surrounding countryside were kept busy for the next few days pulling others who had not been so skillful out of ditches. After making sure we were safe, our parents told us to go to bed because cows still needed to be milked at six a.m. and would not wait because we had been up carousing all night. Ernie and I will never forget our night of driving in "Gumbo Stew" all the way home after the baseball tournament in our hometown.

This was often Father's admonition: "Do not boast about tomorrow, for you do not know what a day may bring forth. Let another praise you and not your own mouth; someone else and not your own lips. Stone is heavy and sand a burden, but provocation by a fool is heavier than both" (Proverbs 27:1-3), along with "A man who loves wisdom brings joy to his father" (Proverbs 29:3a).

Today, I am happy to say that my brother is indeed a wise man with many children and grandchildren who love him, and I also have children who are the love of my life. I have taken up my Mother's tradition of leaving a light in the window if everyone is not safely at home when I go to bed here in the Foothills of Alberta. Here one can also find deposits of that slimy soil which, although rich in nutrients for growing crops, can wreak havoc for builders when trying to erect stable structures—a lesson I learned when I was building my new house. But that's another story!

How Ron Saved the Bonspiel

A story dedicated to small town curlers everywhere.

"If your grades show some marked improvement by the end of the month and stay that way, you will be rewarded in November," Mr. Foster, our eighth-grade teacher, decreed.

"What is the reward?" Ron wanted to know. He was a big boy, good-natured, and fun to be around.

"That is for me to know and you to find out," Mr. Foster replied.

So began a month of hard work and much study. We took Mr. Foster's promise of a reward seriously. He was known for his artful ability to get us out of the stuffy, old classrooms and onto something much more interesting. For instance, the year before he ordered a special rubber-coated baseball when he found us enthusiastically playing ball well after snow had begun to fall. Then he had made a video of the hilarious sight of kids digging like gophers for that ball in a foot of snow in order to stop a home run. As a surprise for our parents, he ran the movie as part of the Christmas concert while we all sang carols. "Only in small town Saskatchewan!" the parents commented after the show.

At the end of October, all of our grades had improved by several percentage points, and the day of revelation and celebration was at hand. Mr. Foster led us on a field trip down the street to the curling rink. Inside the front observation area, the air was blue with cigarette smoke. I couldn't see how this could be a healthy experience, but lucky for us, smoking was not allowed on the ice. There, the air was cool and clean as we assembled to hear our instructions. Mr. Foster revealed that he had made arrangements for us to learn how to curl. Some of the older men who were avid curlers had volunteered their time and expertise to teach us the rules and to demonstrate the finer points of the game.

We were given one hour every day for two weeks to learn the sport. At the end of the instruction, we would form teams and play a round robin tournament in order to find the best players. Those students would then form a team to compete against the two other towns from our school district that were our greatest adversaries in every sport. If we won that bonspiel, we would go on to regional's and have the opportunity to go all the way to the Provincial Youth Curling Championships in Regina.

The fun began. We learned to throw those heavy granite rocks and put a spin on them so they would end up where the skip, or captain of the team, wanted them. We also learned how to sweep so that the brooms would polish the ice and create a clear path for the rock to follow.

The skip was usually someone who was older, larger, and knew more about the game than the rest of the team. Ron became the skip for our team because he had spent plenty of time at the rink, as both his mother and father curled throughout the winter, and had even stood in if someone couldn't make it for a game. He would tell us his strategy, and to us inexperienced players, he became the Supreme Ruler. We tried really hard to follow his demands to curl our rocks to the exact spot he wanted them, and then we swept. I think we even heard his booming command, "SWEEP! SWEEP!" echoing in our heads in our sleep.

That old clapboard curling rink rang with good-natured banter between the students and our coaches throughout the month of November. At the end of the month, Mr. Foster and the volunteer coaches chose two teams from all the students to participate in the area competition. Ron was chosen as one of the skips, and I was to be the lead on his team. Although I didn't have much knowledge or experience at the sport, the men said I had a strong arm and a steady hand. I thought, *Yeah, I have a strong arm from helping Dad throw feed to the cattle and a steady hand from all the painting I did last summer.* But I was really excited, because I was not really good at any other sport. I was too short for the races and the jumping events at track and field, and although I loved a good baseball game, I never learned how to throw or catch a baseball successfully. I hardly slept from excitement.

Even Dad came to watch while we curled every day that week. Finally, after a grueling third game with an extra end, we were declared victorious. We were wound as tight as tops, knowing that we were going on to the next round of competition. Ron almost knocked me off my feet when he came sliding down the ice like a fast-moving curling rock himself to congratulate his team. We were so excited and made plans to wear our school colours for the bonspiel against the other schools from the surrounding towns.

The bonspiel was held at our rink, so we had home ice advantage. The games began on a clear, cold morning, and everyone was in fine form. The competition was stiff, as some of the students from the other towns had been curling for a couple of years, but we were still in the running on the second to the last day.

The weather, however, was not cooperating. You see, we curled on natural ice, not manmade sheets that stayed in perfect condition no matter what the temperature. That day, the weatherman announced that a high-pressure system was moving into the area, bringing one of the rare Chinooks across the plains. Let me explain: Chinooks are winds warmed by the water currents that flow up the coast from California and over the mountains, causing the temperature to rise rather suddenly by several degrees. This phenomenon is usually confined to the foothills of Alberta, but once in a long while, the system is strong enough for the winds to blow all that warm air out onto the great plains of Saskatchewan all the way to our little hometown twenty some miles east of the Alberta border. To our horror, this was one of those occasions, and by last rock of that day, the ice was heavy and sticky. Everyone else in the countryside was happy to have relief from the cold weather, but we were devastated. This was our big chance to beat our rivals and perhaps even go on to the next round of competition, but what were we to do when the predicted high for the next day was to be ten degrees above Fahrenheit?

That night, Ron had a plan to save the ice and soon had a group of the men and boys organized to haul bales of hay from the farms near town. They stacked the bales around the outside of the building to form a thick layer, insulating the building from the sun and wind. Then Ron rounded up some fans that he set in the doors and windows and turned them on only after the temperature dropped for the night. They watched anxiously as the ice began to firm up and dry off after a little grooming.

With shouts of "Keep the doors shut!" and "Come in, and leave the warm air outside!" we began the final game of the bonspiel early the next morning. As the skips changed positions before the last end, we discussed our strategy. The ice was really heavy by this time, and the rocks were not even curling anymore. Ron advised us to give it all we had to get our rocks all the way down the ice to the house. "Don't worry about position so much. Just throw 'em on down!"

We all tried our best, but by the end of that end, the house looked like a parking lot! When it was finally time for the two skips to throw their last rocks, the ice was in terrible shape! They surveyed the scene and removed all the rocks except the counters and the three that lay as guards up front of the house. The opposing skip had the second to the last shot and managed to get one between the guards, laying it in close as a counter. It was well protected, and he had demonstrated his skill as he had managed to get it to curl in behind one of the guards in spite of the terrible ice conditions.

Ron had final rock. We all held our breath and muttered a little prayer as he looked down the mushy expanse of ice at the devastation that awaited him. He took a deep breath, took rock in hand, cleaned the bottom, and raised it slowly back in a wide arc. Then pushing it forward with superhuman strength, he let it go to glory or shame, we knew not which. We ran alongside with our brooms at the ready, but it was no use trying to sweep. We could see the rock pushing a little wake of slush as it went, and to our surprise, it had enough speed that it seemed to hydroplane on that wet surface. In fact, it seemed to be gaining momentum as it neared the house as if going downhill. It cruised on through the guards with a mighty crack, sending them sailing in both directions, continuing on into the house, and took out all the rocks in its path, even the other skip's, until it sat alone to everyone's disbelief like the King of the Castle, right on the button!

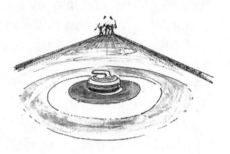

There was a moment's silence, and then total pandemonium broke out as we threw our gold-and-purple toques in the air, whooping and hollering as if we were demented. We all did a happy dance around Ron out there on the slushy ice as students from both schools poured out onto the ice. After the noise died down, the two principals called everyone to attention over the speaker system, and we all made our way to the front of the building for the award ceremony.

Our team stood beaming with pride as we were awarded the trophy and pennant we would carry back to our school. At the end, the manager of the rink came to the podium and called Ron back up. He explained that they had taken up a collection from the crowd watching the bonspiel, and in recognition of the hard work Ron had done and the dedication he had shown while organizing the people who had hauled the bales and set up the fans to save the ice for the bonspiel, they were giving him the money to do whatever he wished. The crowed cheered and stamped their feet calling out, "Speech! Speech!"

Ron took the microphone and very humbly said, "Thank you, everyone, but what I would really like to do with this money is to start a fund so we can build a new, modern rink so future students can have fun like we did today." With that, he handed the envelope back to the manager to the sound of more cheering. Finally, someone started singing, "For he's a jolly good fellow, for he's a jolly good fellow." Some of the bigger boys hoisted him onto their shoulders and carried him all the way back to school.

That was the one and only time I curled in a bonspiel of any importance. I have lost touch with Ron and the other members of the team, but the memory still brings tears to my eyes and a sense of pride in that little town and the good fellows like Ron who lived there.

"The desire of the righteous ends only in good. One man gives freely, yet gains even more . . . A generous man will prosper . . . He who refreshes others will himself be refreshed" (Proverbs 11:23a, 24a, 25).

No Common Woman

This year, 2002, Mom went to be with the Lord. This is a very personal story about her influence on my life.

I come from a long line of women who were compulsive about making the most mundane, mediocre event into something extraordinary and significant. My mother, her sisters, and many of her friends believed that every day could be special and only required a little extra effort on their part to make it so.

I gather that this attitude was passed on to my mother and her siblings from my grandmother, who also was a bit of a Super Mom. Although Grandma cared for and fed a family of fifteen children on a busy farm, she still found the energy and the where-with-all to entertain half the neighborhood after the church service at lunch, and she and her daughters would feed everyone again after the Sunday baseball game for which my grandfather was always the umpire.

Every situation that I remember began with Mom in the kitchen cooking. Lots and lots and lots of cooking! She was an excellent cook and loved to see people eat well, whether it was an everyday meal or a special event. Take, for instance, Sunday, any Sunday. Preparations began with a trip to town on Friday for groceries, where she usually tried to buy something tropical, such as bananas, pineapple, mandarin oranges, or at least something that we could not raise on the farm. Although we were as poor as the mice that lived in our little country church, I never remember going hungry. We always planted huge gardens and preserved hundreds of jars of fruit and vegetables as well as homemade sausage and other meat because we did not have freezers back then. Mother was never satisfied that she had done her best to make the Sunday meal special until she had produced a new salad or found a special way to cook chicken. She would peruse the recipe books and magazines to find at least one "exotic" dish she could make for our meal along with the regular meat, potatoes, and common vegetables. The table groaned with tasty food and so did her guests, who could not resist just one more helping.

Then there was her attitude about cleaning. Saturday morning, a time when a hardworking student would really have appreciated a few extra minutes of sleep, was designated for major cleaning and overhauling of the house, which, by the way, was already clean and tidy. The call "Rise and shine!" would come early, as all bed linens had to be changed before noon and the furniture waxed and polished. Then drawers were to be cleaned out and put in order, with everything folded according to Mother's specifications. Finally, every square inch of the room had to be scrubbed, dusted, and polished, including windows and mirrors, doors and floors, baseboards and knickknacks. If company was coming on Sunday, each bed was bedecked with a special pillows adorned with a three-inch frill of Mom's hand-crocheted lace that had been starched within an inch of its life. When we were finished cleaning each room, if it met with Mother's standards, the door was closed, and no one was allowed to enter again until after the Saturday evening bath ritual.

When we were all squeaky clean and our hair had been washed and put up in anticipation of Sunday services, we were finally allowed to dismantle those lovely beds. We would carefully remove those frilly pillows and the beautiful bedspread, laying them aside to be put back in place before we left for church on Sunday morning. Then at long last, we would creep between the freshly ironed sheets that held the unforgettable scent of cotton washed in Tide with a bit of bleach, starched and line-dried in the rarified, sun-drenched prairie air. I didn't stand a chance at that point. The languor that comes over one after the labours of the workday further augmented by the warmth of a relaxing bath made sleep inevitable as I slipped between soft-scented bedding. That ritual was the best sleeping pill ever invented. I'm sure I was asleep within seconds of my head coming to rest on those plump, feather pillows.

In all the years since, I have yet to find a combination of modern sedative and cleaning products to reproduce the exact smell of that line-dried bedding and the dreamless sleep that came after a Saturday spent cleaning with my mother in that little prairie house.

Laundry was another thing of great pride to Mother. White clothing was bleached, rinsed in water to which bluing had been added, and hung in the sun to dry, which made it so white it hurt your eyes. Most articles of clothing got their fair share of starch, which made my father protest as he struggled with collars even on his work shirts. He once made the comment in jest that he was surprised that Mother didn't starch his boxer shorts. Mother always laid out his Sunday clothing on the freshly made bed, so the next Sunday, she laid out his suit, white shirt, and a pair of boxer shorts that had been starched so stiff that they stood up by themselves.

Sunday always began early, as there were chores to be done before Sunday service. This is why I am still an early riser who appreciates the stillness of the morning before the cares of the day encroach. The cows had to be milked and all the animals fed before we could leave, but Mother always managed to make a special breakfast. She was an efficiency expert when it came to time management and often produced gourmet meals in record time. We each had our share of work to do and did it willingly, if we knew what was good for us. Mother and Dad did not believe in spanking as a form of punishment, but facing their disappointment when we fell short of their standards was more than enough penalty.

If company was coming home with us after church or Mother suspected relatives might drop in, we had the extra chores of making sure the bedrooms and living room had not one stitch of crusty lace out of place before we left and not one speck of dust survived her final inspection. We did not have a telephone in those days, but Mother had an uncanny sixth sense that sent her into a frenzy of preparation for the imminent arrival of guests. And she was usually right.

Houses were small and simple in those post-World War II days, so the younger females and boys would entertain their friends outside or in their bedrooms, while the men occupied the living room, and the ladies spent their time together in the kitchen. Therefore, the state of their handiwork and the polish on the floors became for them a reflection of their work ethic and about the only status symbols those prairie housekeepers could afford.

My mother was a pro at changing sugar bags combined with miles and miles of crotchet cotton into works of art. During the cold winter evenings while the blizzards raged over the Saskatchewan prairies, she would sit tucked under a patchwork quilt next to the oil heater that dominated our tiny living room in winter, working on her latest project. Her nimble fingers, holding the crotchet hook or needle, worked as quickly as a well-oiled machine to produce miles of lace and doilies for tables. She would make dresses, other clothing, and baby shawls out of fine wool and sweaters with booties and hats to match. The hook would wink and flash in the light of the coal oil lamp as her hands flew from chain stitch to double stitch, creating a work of art out of a ball of string.

In 1962, we had a complete crop failure. In those days, we were so poor we only used one lamp in the evening, so we would all huddle together around the oil heater in the living room. Yet I remember those evenings spent with Dad and Mother as very special. Looking back, I know that those times, although we had little by way of worldly goods, laid the foundation of who I am and what I do today. Dad would read to us from the Bible or *National Geographic*, sharing bits of particularly relevant knowledge, while Mom's needles never missed a stitch and I worked at my lessons. Since becoming an adult, I have learned to appreciate both the craft of needlework from Mom and the joy of reading from Dad. These hobbies, which have also become my source of income, not only produce something useful and beautiful but are also therapeutic. I tend to forget the cares of the day when I am counting stitches or lose myself between the pages of a good book.

Mom approached each day as a day unto itself, working tirelessly to produce the best life she could for her husband and children. She often said, "Never trouble Trouble until Trouble troubles you," which I believe is a loose translation of Matthew 6:34 that says each day has enough trouble for its self. Even though she had little to give, she worked tirelessly on charity projects the ladies aid group of our church participated in, making baby layettes for the hospital in the Congo or rolling bandages from worn-out sheets for army hospitals.

Mom lived with a kind of optimistic excitement running through her veins. I believe she acquired that attitude from her parents, who held the belief that anything was possible when you were willing to dream, believe, and work hard to achieve your goals. She always made something beautiful or useful out of the ordinary and spared no effort in making a comfortable, beautiful home using the least expensive products. She made clothing on the old treadle Singer sewing machine using fabric salvaged from some relative's cast-off clothing or draperies from fabric ordered from the Eaton's catalogue. The same applied to the meals she prepared. The simple dinners shared by our family were always just as tasty as the feast she prepared for forty relatives who happened to drop in on a Sunday to visit. Mother not only coped but also excelled at any and all of these tasks.

One particular blue dress made of silk organza will always be the symbol of her love and commitment to me. She made this dress for the Easter Sunday of my thirteenth year. It took hours and hours of her precious time to make this complicated dress, which was more like a ball gown. Having no pattern, she used as her guide a picture of the dress I had found in a magazine and had fallen in love with. Being thirteen and very self-centered, I did not appreciate that she did this during the busiest time of year on the farm—spring planting. I was so disappointed when it was still not finished at ten o'clock on Saturday evening when I was sent to bed. Yet there it hung on my door, completed and pressed, when I awoke the next morning.

I believe Mother finished the miles of hemming on that bouffant skirt by lamplight at about two in the morning. Although it must have taken her last ounce of energy and a great deal of willpower to complete the dress, she would never have of disappointing me by saying, "I can't finish this." She was a self-starter who needed no one to tell her what needed to be done and seldom gave up on a project once she had made a commitment.

Mother often talked about the skills and methods her own mother and father had taught their large family with a kind of reverence that comes from watching someone achieve the extraordinary with few resources. They had been poor immigrants who left their extended family and creature comforts behind in the Ukraine to carve out a new life on the hostile Canadian plains. My grandfather was a self-taught doctor, who could set bones and became somewhat of a legend for his skills. My grandmother was a wonderful cook and loving mother who passed those skills onto her daughters. Society talks of genetic memory as that which passes survival skills from one generation to the next, and I believe our family is better off because the chain connecting the generations is strong.

Mother believed that if you didn't know how to do something you could learn it from a book, the radio, a sister, or an aunt. In her later years, she credited her own children with encouraging her to keep on learning as they expanded their horizons and hers along with them. She was a lifelong learner with a determination to succeed no matter what life threw in her path; the more difficult the project, the more determined she became. I watched her live well into her eighty-ninth year, and the glint of determination and excitement never left her until ill health took away her independence. But even on the last evening of her life, she taught me how to end well as she asked me to repeat the Lord's Prayer with her before she slipped into a coma.

When presented with a challenge, I feel the same determination that Mother did and attribute my work ethic and perseverance through difficult times to her example. I learned from her that the feeling of satisfaction that comes from achieving your goal no matter what the odds and doing your best for those you love is the only reward worth working for on this earth. This is what this most uncommon woman, although only a poor, Saskatchewan homemaker with an eighth-grade education, passed on to my siblings and me by her example.

I can think of no better description for my mother than Proverbs 31:10-31:

> A wife of noble character, who can find? She is worth far more than rubies. Her husband has full confidence in her and lacks for nothing of value. She brings him good, not harm, all the days of her life. She selects wool and flax and works with eager hands. She is like the merchant ships, bringing her food from afar. She gets up while it is still dark; she provides food for her family and portions for her servant girls. She considers a field and buys it; out of her earnings she plants a vineyard. She sets about her

work vigorously; her arms are strong for their tasks. She sees that her trading is profitable, and her lamp does not go out at night. In her hand she holds the distaff and grasps the spindle with her fingers. She opens her arms to the poor and extends her hands to the needy. When it snows, she has no fear for her household; for all of them are clothed in scarlet. She makes coverings for her bed; she is clothed in fine linen and purple. Her husband is respected at the city gate, where he takes his seat among the elders of the land. She makes linen garments and sells them, and supplies the merchants with sashes. She is clothed with strength and dignity; she can laugh at the days to come. She speaks with wisdom, and faithful instruction is on her tongue. She watches over the affairs of her household and does not eat the bread of idleness. Her children arise and call her blessed; her husband also, and he praises her: "Many women do noble things, but you surpass them all." Charm is deceptive, and beauty is fleeting; but a woman who fears the Lord is to be praised. Give her the reward she has earned, and let her works bring her praise at the city gate.

I believe my father saw these attributes in her and that is why there were married a mere twenty nine days after they had met and were hand holding sweet hearts through good times and bad for forty-nine years until Dad went to be with the Lord in 1980.

A Summer Memory

On a fine summer afternoon when the air was hazy and the neighbor was out cutting the hay my children and I had cleaned the cabin and then went off to the local farmer's Market at the Millarville Race Track. We returned with bags full of fresh vegetables and yummy baking from the fine variety of venders we found there. After lunch everyone including the dog found a comfortable place for a nap. Finding myself the only one awake and thinking of how my Mother had relished a minute of quiet after lunch on the farm in Saskatchewan, this piece of poetry just seemed to write it's self.

A Mother's Minute

Sleepy children go to rest,

For on this day they did their best.

The house is clean. The shopping's done.

The plates are washed. Their prize is won.

A prize so special and so sweet,

A wee, soft pillow is their treat.

Their tired eyes right now they close,

Their hands they fold in soft repose.

The dog, as well, goes to her bed

To join the children, a sleepy head.

As off to dreamland they do fly,

They leave behind each care and sigh.

But soon they'll wake, once more to run,

To carry on their day of fun.

They'll laugh and play, romp and sing.

Then their laughter loud will ring!

But just for now, I have a mother's minute,

To savour silence and my lovely, sleeping children.

A Winter Wash

I remember well my mother's comment, "We are either the cleanest family I know or the dirtiest, and I can't decide which!" as she faced the mountains of dirty laundry our family generated back there on the farm. It was probably her own fault we had so much laundry because her standards regarding our clothing were very high. For instance, she would never allow anyone in the family to wear anything more than one day. Even my father, who worked in the dusty field, would not get out of the house without putting on a clean shirt. He often said that our clothing was worn out from washing, not wearing.

Whenever I hear young women today complaining about having washday blues, I like to tell them about a particular day during the winter of 1961, when we did the laundry after a blizzard out on the farm.

The day dawned cold but calm and clear. The sun shone over the frozen expanse of our yard for the first time in about three weeks. You see, the blizzard had started on January first about noon. Uncle, aunty, and my cousins had come to visit after the church service, and Mom had decided it was a perfect day to cook the fat duck she had been saving for a special occasion.

The bird was just beginning to smell wonderful when Dad and my uncle came in from watering the cows. Uncle came in stamping his boots to issue a command that everyone must get ready to leave immediately. You see, we lived on the Great Plains of Saskatchewan where the country was flat and you could see for miles. When the two men had gone to throw some feed over for the cattle, they were at the highest point in our yard and what they had seen had scared them both. There, to the west, they had seen a long, low mass of gray clouds boiling along the distant horizon. Dad said it looked like a snowstorm being driven by an almighty wind.

It turned out to be a blizzard of massive proportions coming across the prairie straight at us. My mother quickly cut choice pieces from the duck for them to take home with them as well as half of all the other dishes she had prepared. They bundled up with good-byes and good wishes for the New Year, much to the dismay of my cousin, Ilene, and I. You see, we had been planning on doing each other's hair and looking at the latest fashions in the new Eaton's catalogue. We were sad about parting so soon because we didn't get to spend much time together. You see we lived nearly twenty miles apart and especially in the winter when the roads were treacherous and blocked with huge snowdrifts we didn't see each other for months. But today their main concern was making it home to move their cows into the barnyard before the storm struck.

About an hour after they left, the storm enveloped our little farm with the fury of a demon, howling down the chimney like a banshee. The force of the wind whipped the new snow into a frenzy causing a complete whiteout by two o'clock in the afternoon. It was as dark as after sunset, so we lit the coal oil lamps in order to see the food on our plates as we celebrated the New Year, sadly, by ourselves. Mom turned on the radio, but it was hard to hear over the static caused by the driving wind and airborne ice crystals.

For the next twenty-one days, the wind blew with the same unwavering intensity. It was dark morning, noon, and night, and we didn't see another soul, not even a rabbit. The dog would not go out except to accompany Dad to the barn, and I could not go to school seven miles away, as the buses did not run in such weather. By the second day, the roads became impassable and disappeared completely under drifts of snow so hard we could have cut blocks to build an igloo.

To keep our minds off the weather, I read and Mom sewed. We kept the lamp and fire burning, while Dad struggled to keep the cattle from freezing, bringing as many as he could into the barn and the yard and putting out extra deep bedding straw. He had to tie several ropes together with one end attached to the house and the other to the barnyard gate so he could find his way back and forth from the barn to the house without getting lost. If he was out too long, Mom would dress warmly and, following the rope, would check to see if he was okay. You see, you could develop hypothermia in less than an hour in those winds and temperatures, a fact we were well aware of because my father had lost an uncle who had frozen to death while trying to make it home three miles from town during a blizzard. I had never been afraid in a blizzard before, but this one caused all of us concern. I think it was the only time I heard Dad pray out loud for our neighbors, an elderly couple and their son, a veteran of World War II, who lived five miles north of us. They lived in a very old house, and we were afraid such a long, cold stretch would be hard on them.

So it was with great joy that we woke up very early on the twenty-second day, not because someone had set an alarm, but simply because the world was silent once more. Dad got up first, as he always did, to light the fire in the woodstove in the kitchen, and I could hear him and Mom talking. *I could hear them talking!* There was no 'banshee' howling down the chimney and no ice crystals beating against the windowpanes. The old farmhouse was no longer groaning against the force of the wind. All was silent, blessedly silent, except for the odd popping sound of the earth cracking from the extreme cold.

I bounced out of bed and scraped a hole in the frost on the windowpane in the kitchen to see the outdoor thermometer, which read thirty-five below zero Fahrenheit. Beyond it, I saw nothing but blinding white snowdrifts for as far as the eye could see. Fences and bushes were hidden under several feet of snow that looked like whipping cream standing in peaks where once the rolling fields had been.

The dog scratched to get out, but the snow in front of the house had drifted in so deep that we had climb out of the window to cut huge blocks from in front of the door in order to open it. The snow was so hard that the dog didn't even leave tracks on top of it. A huge drift came off the back of the chicken house roof and continued on down the hill over the fence and into the valley. I couldn't wait to bundle up and go out with my sled.

Now, I would have thought that laundry would be the least important thing on my mother's mind that beautiful morning, but that was the next thing she thought of after breakfast. "We are almost out of clean clothing, and you can never tell if the blizzard will start up again, so I want to get the laundry done just in case!" she said with real concern. Because we did not have running water or a water heater, all the water used in the old wringer washer had to be hauled from the well and heated on the old woodstove. So Dad set off with the horse and a flat sled we called a stone boat to haul a barrel of water, and we set about heating it on the stove while sorting the clothing into loads.

Because all the water used in the house had to be carried uphill from the well in pails or hauled up in a barrel, the water for washing clothes was reused for several loads, refreshed by adding a little hot water to each new load. This method conserved water and washing detergent. Mom always washed the most delicate whites first. Next came the tea towels, which she also boiled to disinfect them. Then she washed all the colored clothing and finally the work clothing.

When a load had been washed for the right amount of time, each garment had to be fished out of the hot water, put through the wringers, rinsed in a tub of clean water, and put through the wringers again. You had to fold the wet clothing in such a way that it would feed through the wringers without too many creases or becoming too bulky, which would make the wringers pop open. You also had to be careful not to get your fingers or your hair caught in the wringers because that could do real damage. When all the laundry had been washed and rinsed by hand, it had to be hung on the line to dry.

We had to cut and shovel a path to the clothesline because the snow came halfway up the poles that supported the lines. The temperature that morning was still twenty-five below zero at ten a.m., and the wet clothing began to freeze before we even got it pinned to the line. Our hands froze too, and we were soon chilled to the bone from handling all the wet stuff, making the whole process a really miserable job. The temperature did go up during the few hours of sun we had later in the afternoon, and some of the lighter pieces actually seemed to freeze dry—well, at least partially. Then before evening, we had to remove all the frozen clothing from the line and bring it back into the house where Mom had strung lines from the four corners of the kitchen, making a big X to hang the still-wet pieces.

I helped to carry the frozen laundry in while she pried the clothespins from each piece. Pants and shirts were as stiff as boards, and I could only carry two or three pieces in at a time. I had to be careful not to break off the legs of Dad's pants or the sleeves of his shirts. Dad wore combination underwear in winter, which were like an entire bodysuit with long sleeves and legs, and were the most unwieldy things to carry into the house when frozen stiff, as they were taller than I was and banged against my shins when I navigated the deep drifts. It was like carrying pieces of clothing that had been cut out of a board. We laid it all on the kitchen table near the stove to thaw and then hung it up on the lines. Many of the old wooden clothespins had frozen onto the clothing and could only be removed after thawing in the kitchen. For the next two days, we navigated through the house between dripping wash hanging in the kitchen, living room, and over doors. As it dried, Mom would heat up the old flatiron on the stove to make everything starched and wrinkle-free, smelling for all the world like the great out doors on that cold winter morning, which I will never forget.

I was mighty glad we had done the laundry because on the fourth day after the blizzard, Dad came in saying he could hear a motor coming toward us from the north, which from the sound of it, was our neighbor's son's Jeep.

He soon appeared, coming straight across country because the deep drifts obliterated all the fences and roads. He was on his way to town for supplies with the Jeep and a trailer and suggested that I pack a suitcase and come along if I intended to go to school at all that winter. He speculated that it would be spring before the school bus could navigate the roads once more, and he was right. I packed all those clean clothes and everything else I would need to stay with a family in town. Dad and I hopped into the Jeep for the ride of our lives as we bucked and jumped over snowdrifts all the way to town, which were like sand dunes measuring six- to eight-feet deep and carved into weird shapes by the force of the wind.

My maiden name was Frank, and my friends in school composed a song that they sang to the tune of "Yankee Doodle" that went like this, "Frankie Doodle came to town, riding in a jeep, dear. Stuck a suitcase in the back and came to town to sleep here." I was billeted with the Baptist minister and his family, which suited me fine because they had two daughters my own age.

I didn't see Mom and Dad again until April when they managed to come to town with the horses and wagon, the only means of travel once all that snow began to melt. You can imagine the condition of those gumbo roads. There was more water in the sloughs that year than anyone could remember, and driving was a challenge right up to the time when the school bus finally made it through in the middle of May.

I have a sign in my laundry room next to the washboard Mother used with this quote written upon it, "Cleanliness is next to godliness." Mother definitely believed that, and I do too here and now because I own and operate a dry cleaning plant. I have promised myself that I will never ever complain about doing laundry while I use the modern machines I now own both in my dry cleaning plant and at home. If I hear the young women of today complain about doing laundry using those lovely, shiny, efficient, front-loading, electronically controlled machines they all seem to have these days, I would like to share this story with them.

The Howlin' Smokehouse Blues

I woke early in the gray dawn of that November day to the aroma of coffee and frying pork sausages. Our farmhouse did not have central heating, so when I opened my eyes a crack, I saw there was a thick layer of frost on the bedroom window. The water pail would be frozen in the kitchen this morning, I thought, as I burrowed deeper into the thick down quilt for a few more winks of sleep. Then I heard a lone coyote howling from someplace nearby. *Howlin' at the big full moon last night*, I surmised sleepily. Then I heard an answering howl from the south, and that plus the smell of breakfast made me decide to roll out of bed.

I slipped into a warm housecoat and slippers, defense against the chill morning air and cold floors, and opened the door to the kitchen. A rush of warm air greeted me along with the heavenly aroma of freshly baked breakfast biscuits.

"Good morning!" Mom greeted me. She was always so cheerful and loud in the morning.

"Mornin'," I mumbled, rubbing my eyes and stretching.

"Who's so tired?" she asked. "I'll bet you stayed up late reading again last night, didn't you?" It was a question that did not need a response. My brother and I were both avid readers and famous for reading by the light of the coal oil lamp until the wee hours of the morning.

"Do you want some coffee?" Dad asked. He made this wonderful coffee his mother had made for him when he was a child from half and half, coffee, and hot milk, with a spoonful of brown sugar. The only difference was that when he was young and they were new homesteaders in this country, they couldn't afford real coffee but drank instead a brew made out of roasted wheat and chicory. He had made some for us once, and it wasn't bad.

Mom and Dad were talking about the work we had to do that day. Since it was Saturday, I didn't have school, but I was expected to do my share of chores and housecleaning anyway. They had spent the last two days butchering, so the house had a greasy, garlicky aroma. I knew we would be scrubbing down everything in the kitchen for sure.

While I sat sipping the sweet, hot coffee, I listened to Dad talking to Mom about how he was going to package the sausage he had made and smoked the day before. He had made this ingenious smokehouse out of the old metal jacket that had surrounded the potbelly stove in the one-room schoolhouse called Victory Hill that my siblings had attended. It had closed about the time I was born and the school board had offered everything in the school to the farmers who had helped to build it. So Dad brought some books, a desk for me, and the stove jacket home on the back of the wagon. He set the jacket up near his smithy to make it into a smokehouse. It was ideal, six feet in diameter and seven feet high, made in segments of heavy steel with a door on one side that allowed the teacher to feed wood into the potbelly stove that sat inside of it.

After Dad brought it home, he created a roof for it out of sheet metal with a small hole in the centre to act as chimney. Then he threaded pieces of metal rod through it from side to side near the top on which he could hang sausages and hams from his latest round of butchering. Last, he made a fire pit in the bottom out of gravel. When he had finished, he stood back and looked at it with real pride, having made a useful article out of what could have been junk.

We usually butchered in the late fall once the weather was cool enough so that the animal could hang for a short time. This time, Dad had decided to butcher both a steer and a pig so that they could make the fine sausages he was famous for. It was not an easy job and needed a skilled person who knew how to make the best cuts into roasts and steaks. Then the remaining meat would be deboned and ground through a small hand grinder to make hamburger. I had helped to turn the handle of the meat grinder, an exercise in patience and muscle building. Some of that ground beef would then be mixed with ground pork and seasoning to make the sausages we all loved. It was time consuming and strenuous work that took at least two to three days to complete. Today, the work was almost finished, with only the cleanup and packaging left. Well, at least that was what Dad and Mom thought.

When we sat down to breakfast, the frost had thawed off the kitchen window so we could see the driveway that came into the yard and into the field beyond. The sun was up and everything was sparkling with hoarfrost. As we took the first bites of breakfast, a coyote came trotting down the driveway not more than ten feet from the house. Dad stood up and leaned over to watch him pass, exclaiming, "What in the world is a coyote doing so close to the house?" When he tried to open the kitchen door, the poor old collie was pressed up against the door so tightly that Dad had to push with all his might to open it even a crack. As soon as there was a space wide enough to allow the dog to pass through, he scrambled in, almost knocking Dad over in the process. He slunk under the table and sat there, shaking and whining. By now, Dad was really concerned and grabbed the rifle from its rack before stepping out onto the porch.

Dad stood for a minute, allowing his eyes to adjust to the bright light and then began to count, "One, two, three, four, five."

Mom stepped outside and asked, "What are you counting?"

"Coyotes!" was his simple answer.

"Why are there so many coyotes around? Did you leave something from the butchering out that attracted them?" Mom asked in an accusing tone.

"No! I hauled all that stuff down to the dump a mile away!" Dad snapped. Just then, a gust of wind came from the northeast, bringing with it the scent of smoked meat. "Ah ha!" said Dad. "They came for the sausage. I'll bet they can smell it five miles away!"

You see, we had finished making the sausage really late the previous afternoon, and Dad had hung it and the hams in the smokehouse over the small fire he had built out of hickory and apple wood branches he had been saving for just that purpose. He allowed it to smoke for about two to three hours and then checked it and dampened down the coals about midnight. Because everything was still so hot, he thought—I repeat, he thought—that it would be fine to leave everything as it was to cool overnight. He had come in declaring the job was done, the fire was out, and he was very tired. He had gone off to bed for a well-deserved rest. But little did he know that a few hot coals had survived the damping and, fed by the dripping grease from the hot sausages, they had flared up into a small bonfire. This in turn made the sausages drip even more, which caused the fire to burn higher and making the hams drip.

Well, I think you can guess the rest of the story! When Dad tried to open the door of the smokehouse, it was so hot he couldn't touch it. That was his first clue to the disaster that awaited him when he wrapped an old rag around his hand and jerked the door open. He let out a strangled scream then, for all that was left of the meat he had hung the day before was one tiny piece of blackened ham the size of a baseball and two shriveled black sausages. All the rest were lying burnt on the still-smoking coals that were glowing and winking red like the eyes of some evil demon from its bed in the bottom of the famous smokehouse. Dad almost fainted then, and Mom couldn't believe her eyes. She just put her arms around him, and they stood for a long time, just holding each other in the thin, cold morning air. It was really hard watching a man like my Dad cry, as he was always so firm and sure of himself. But that day, he shed tears for the loss of the meat we had counted on to feed us through the cold winter months, and for the hard work we had all done to produce the sausage. Many years later, he admitted he also shed tears for his own stupidity.

The sausage was gone, but at least we had the answer as to why there was a coyote sitting on every hill around the farm that morning. Over the next couple of weeks, Dad set out to shoot those coyotes with a vengeance, partially out of concern for the safety of the rest of the herd of cattle. However, later I learned that there was a bounty paid by the provincial government for coyotes because they had become very prolific for about two years, forming large packs that invaded the cattle and sheep herds in the surrounding countryside. With the money Dad received from the bounty, he bought another yearling pig and half of a steer from my uncle to replace the lost meat. Until the meat supply was replaced, Dad wore a very long face and seldom laughed. It took years for Dad to overcome the blues from that incident because he blamed himself. Finally, he let it go and was able laugh when he told the story about the day the smokehouse burned and the coyotes howled.

I don't know what happened to that smokehouse. Maybe Dad sold it to the scrap dealer who came though the neighborhood looking for scrap metal. All I know is that he never used it again after that to smoke sausage.

I thought of this incident the other evening when my son came home proudly holding a bag of freshly smoked venison sausage he and his friends had made. Later, I read these verses in Proverbs 15: 33 and continue through chapter16; 1 and 2 that seemed like an exclamation point to the story:

"The fear of the Lᴏʀᴅ teaches a man wisdom, but humility comes before honour. To man belong the plans of the heart, but from the Lᴏʀᴅ comes the reply of the tongue. All a man's ways seem innocent to him, but motives are weighed by the Lᴏʀᴅ."

How I Spent My Summer Vacation

The summer I turned sixteen, I embarked on what for me became a life-changing summer vacation. My brother had married and was the manager of McFarland Lumber in High River, near the foothills of Alberta. He and his wife invited me to come for an extended visit during my summer vacation, and he even offered to pay me for helping him with some of the paperwork in his busy office. While I was working there, two events took place that changed me forever.

Soon after I arrived in High River and began working at the lumberyard, a nice-looking local boy asked me to go to the movies with him. This would have been my first date if my brother had allowed me to go, but he did not because the young man was twenty-one. Being very protective of his kid sister, my brother asked him, "Do you have any idea how old this little lady is?" Then he informed that nice young man that he would be robbing the cradle, so he had better go find someone his own age. That experience, however, was an awakening of sorts, as I became aware of my own appearance and boys for the first time.

The second and most important event of that summer was my chance meeting with the author, W. O. Mitchell. He was born in Weyburn, Saskatchewan, which coincidentally was my stepfather's hometown as well. Although he was just a common prairie boy, he had the ability to write stories about his youthful adventures that were at once funny and nostalgic. I grew to admire and enjoy his work while listening to the radio series *Jake and the Kid* that had been on CBC radio from 1950-1956, the years before I started school. In fifth grade, his book *Who Has Seen the Wind* was required reading for all Saskatchewan students and was one of my favourites.

Mr. Mitchell had written many other stories and gave public readings of his work, which drew large audiences because the amusing stories of his years growing up on the prairies filled people with nostalgia. His work had also been made into a series for television, and he was often called the Mark Twain of Canada because of his vivid descriptions of the lives and adventures of young boys. Besides being a prolific writer, he was a respected teacher across the prairies and had received many awards and honorary degrees for his work. The highest honour was the award that made him an Officer of the Order of Canada in 1973. So now you may understand why I, a budding writer, was a little in awe of this man and why I was so excited to meet him.

The introduction occurred on an ordinary morning in July when W. O., or Bill, as most people around there called him, came storming into my brother's office saying he had some cheeky sparrows nesting in his living room! After further conversation, my brother learned that the fireplace chimney attached to his house just west of High River had begun to lean at a precarious angle away from the rest of the house, leaving a gap between the wall and the chimney, which said cheeky sparrows had taken full advantage of that spring.

My brother had had dealings with this crusty old curmudgeon before and so was not surprised when he turned up asking for supplies and advice as to how to solve the problem. I was extremely shy when my brother first introduced me to him; after all, this was a great man in my eyes. In the days following, Bill turned up often, looking for supplies. Once he even came on a Sunday morning, looking for sixteen bags of cement, as the project to lift the chimney and pour a footing of concrete under it became a bigger challenge than they had at first thought. I learned on that Sunday morning as my brother and I went off to church, leaving Bill to find the cement on his own, that he lived in his own world as writers often do, not conscious of the time of day or the days of the week.

If my brother was busy with another client, which he often was, Bill would wait in the office, where he entertained me with his stories. He was the inveterate storyteller and would often pull up a nail keg—you know, one of those old wooden ones—for a stool, sit, close his eyes, fold his arms, and embark on some tale of adventure that kept me and anyone else who happened into the office spellbound for its duration.

In those days, all businesses closed for the noon hour, and so the men from out of town were obliged to eat out if they wished to finish their business later. Across the street from the lumberyard was a restaurant owned and operated by Donnie Yip. We were acquainted with the Yip family, as Donnie had relatives who ran a market garden near Medicine Hat. Donnie was sometimes my brother's hunting partner and a character, as well as a restaurateur who served pretty good food. So during that summer, we often had our noon meal in Donnie's restaurant. It was there that I was privileged to hear the story "How I Spent My Summer Holidays" as only Bill Mitchell could deliver it.

He embarked on the story of that youthful misadventure, demonstrating the logistics of the yard and the ensuing explosion by using his plate to represent the house, the sugar dispenser as the outhouse, the knives for the clothesline poles, and the other utensils to represent the wood pile. I have never forgotten that rare, wonderful performance by that animated, keen writer. Bill was always very humble about his ability to share stories, and for me it was a real privilege to spend a summer close to this talented and intelligent man. He is one of the people most influential in inspiring and encouraging me to tell my own stories. That summer in the foothills, I discovered that I *liked* boys, but I *loved* to hear good stories. When I returned home, Mom and Dad recognized that I had changed. I had matured and was more interested in my appearance, asking to use makeup and becoming a better student as well. In fact, I achieved honour standings in my final exams that year, which I attribute to the experiences of my summer vacation and my tenth-grade teacher, Mr. Carl Ast.

I found our little community had changed as well. Our little farmhouse was in a state of chaos because it was being wired for electricity. Yes, we were *finally*, in the year 1965, going to have electricity installed on our farm and the neighboring farms as well. This was a real victory after the disputes we had had about the placement of the poles with our neighbor to the south, who had held up the process for years. You see, Saskatchewan Power did not follow the roads when installing the power poles. In order to save poles, the power line was installed straight across country from one house to the next by the shortest route, making it difficult for a farmer to cultivate his fields. After years of discussions with that stubborn neighbor and others like him, the provincial government finally passed a bill making the arbitrary decision that the line must go through so that all citizens would have equal access to this modern convenience. So all our lives changed dramatically that summer, as we were finally able to watch TV, use modern appliances, and power tools.

That was also the last summer I lived at home on the farm. Our high school did not have enough students left to attract and pay for a good teacher, so off I went to the city where I lived with my older sister, Ethel and her family for two years. There I attended a large high school, found a husband, had two lovely children, and a business career. My life changed drastically as the big city swallowed me whole and didn't spit me out again until I was fifty-two.

During those years while living in the city, I was privileged to attend many functions where W. O. Mitchell was the guest speaker, during which he would share some new and exciting adventure as only he could tell it. Once having the opportunity to speak to him, I told him I was interested in writing and had the audacity to ask for his advice. All he said was, "Just begin, sweetie! It's like jumping out of a plane. You can't have the experience until you jump, and then you just let yourself free fall. Just jump! You'll find your own style and learn from it." He inspired many writers to "just jump and free fall" with his gruff confidence.

Another time, after one of his weekend seminars at the Banff School of Fine Arts, I heard him say that if you are truly a storyteller, you have to let the story out or you'll choke. During one of his last public appearances, when he told the story of how he came by his first pair of long pants, he said, "If you have thoughts, you better pen them down because they're like wild horses and will run away!" He was always full of colourful phrases that stayed with you and made you think.

Today, because my memory sometimes fails me, I too have learned to pen my thoughts down. It's not surprising that I have become a storyteller now that I have a little more time to write in these later years of my life, having returned to the country where I am able to appreciate the simple life and slow down once more.

During a sermon one Sunday, as we were studying the life of Christ and his method of teaching the multitudes, I realized that storytelling is a calling given by God. You see, we learned that Christ was the ultimate and supreme storyteller, who is in fact called the Word! In John 1:1-3 we are told, "In the beginning was the Word and the Word was with God and the Word was God," and in John 1:14 we learn that "The Word became flesh and lived for a while among us. We have seen his glory, the glory of the one and only Son, who came from the Father, full of grace and truth." In order to impart that grace and truth to us, he employed a form of storytelling called parables, which we still study today to learn the will of the Father.

So this year, I spent my summer vacation compiling these stories into book form, which I hope will bring you some humour, entertainment, and inspiration.

PART II

Show me, O Lord, my life's end
And the number of my days;
Let me know how fleeting is my life.
You have made my life a mere hand-breadth;
The span of my years is as nothing before you.
Each man's life is but a breath. Selah.
He bustles about, but only in vain;
he heaps up wealth, not knowing
who will get it.
But now, Lord, what do I look for?
My hope is in you!
—Psalm 39: 4-7

Prologue II

New Memories

I once heard someone say, "Life is what happens while you're busy making other plans".

So it is that the woman who returned to the little town in Saskatchewan in 1979 was a much different person than the girl who had left for the city thirteen years before.

I had left with so many plans and dreams. I had planned to complete High School and I had dreamed of achieving a teaching degree allowing me to teach handicapped children. Yes, I had also dreamt of the tall good looking husband, the house and two children but those dreams had never included the nightmare of a divorce and becoming a single mother, without having finished the education I needed to be self-sufficient. Good heavens, I didn't even have a driver's license! So, that summer when I returned to Golden Prairie for the reunion I was devastated and felt like a total failure before God, my family and my old friends from home. The question that reigned supreme in my mind that summer consisted of one word, "Why?" and to expand that question: Why would a loving God, whom I had known since my earliest years, allow this to happen to me and my children? Of what earthly good could I be if my spiritual life, my emotions and my reputation were in tatters?

The answer was to come gradually while I worked with other women over the next few years who, like myself, had suffered the defeat of a divorce and were struggling to feed and care for their children on a very limited budget; both of money and time as they were poorly paid working mothers.

They often worked two or three jobs to provide for their children. many had little or no education and very little support from family or community. One day after an argument with my boss regarding better wages and some dental benefits for the staff he said these words to me, "You can be replaced. There are a hundred more like you outside my door!" It was because of those words that I came to understand the lesson God was patiently teaching me. The answer also consisted of one word, "Humility!" The answer was that I needed to let go of everything, my dreams and hopes and the achievements I had been so proud of and simply throw myself at Christ's feet in utter and absolute humility.

I am happy to report that after much struggle things improved and the following stories are the fruit of the lessons I have allowed God to teach me. These days I define success as the ability to do the best I can with what is in front of me right now and security is having three or four unread books on my shelf! All I ask for is love and patience because I know He, my Lord and Master, is not finished with me yet. I have learned to cling to the promises of God like the one found in Proverbs 3:25 and 26; Have no fear of sudden disaster or of the ruin that overtakes the wicked, for the Lord will be your confidence and will keep your foot from being snared.

The Reunion

We drove into town from the east on that fine Canada Day in 1979. The sun was shining brightly as we bumped over the familiar hump of the now defunct railway tracks. We drove up the main street past the grain elevators standing still and quiet, retired sentinels of a past era. At the intersection where First Street joined Railway Ave we turned the corner at the General Store toward the Community Hall.

The place had not changed much in the thirteen years since I had left this town and the farm I had called home. There were fewer businesses operating, but the buildings were still there, low, squat structures built in the style of the turn of the century with false fronts to make them appear more grandiose than they really were. Their wooden siding had long since been weathered into a kind of monotone gray, but here and there were a few that had been newly painted in honour of the day we had come to celebrate.

Mom, Dad, my two youngsters, and I had come home to celebrate the town's fiftieth anniversary. Banners hung in front of the community hall, and a sign said, "Welcome Home." Cars and trucks were parked everywhere, and people of all ages were outside the hall, milling about and setting up a stage with a microphone and speakers as well as chairs in rows for the ecumenical church service that would kick-off the day's events.

Just as we found a parking place near the old school yard, a whirlwind of fine proportions came spinning down the side street from the opposite direction, lifting dust and debris from the street as it passed by. Then it turned the corner as if it had an invisible driver and went up the side street, where it finally went off the road into the Caragana hedge that bordered the old school yard. After lifting a few old gum wrappers and lost pages from someone's notebook out of the bushes, it finally lost steam and settled in the playground as quickly as it had started. Dad said, "That was a fine 'welcome home'!" He slammed the car door. "It still looks the same. Dry and windy!"

As we walked in front of the hall where the church service was to take place, we heard the Baptist minister announce that volunteers were needed for the mass choir that would be singing at the service. Mom pushed me forward and said, "Here is one!" just as two of my old friends walked up to join.

For the rest of the day, we visited with old friends, shared a wonderful barbeque, and watched one of that area's famous baseball games. Some of the players were a little older and slower, but the cheering was just as enthusiastic and the catcalls were just as caustic. After the game, we were invited to tour the school where we saw the trophies we had won and artwork we had done before we had left for adventure in the big, wide world. Then we all trouped back to the community hall where the ladies of the town served their famous chicken dinner that brought back memories of our childhood. The day's conversations were rife with phrases, such as "Remember when . . . ?" and "Do you still sing?" Or, "Do you still draw?"

I had left the community thirteen years before to go to school with never a backward glance. In those days I couldn't leave that town in the rearview mirror fast enough! That was at age sixteen. Now here I was at age twenty-nine, with my heart a little battered from a marriage that had ended badly and a lot wiser than I had been at sixteen. That day, my broken heart began to mend and my soul learned how to sing again as I listened to the chatter of old friends and the sound of the prairie wind playing its familiar tune in the wires. No matter what had happened I was still accepted here for who I really was and I was grounded once more.

We sat visiting until the sun began to set and my father, who was pushing eighty, said he needed to go back to my Aunt's house to rest. He stooped to pick up a little soil before we got into the car and let it filter through his fingers with a faraway look in his eyes. We didn't know at the time that that would be his last trip home. He often sat with my children after that visit, telling them stories of his younger years.

They say you can never go home again. I don't know who "they" are, but I know a piece of my heart will always be with those friends and that little town on the prairies of Saskatchewan, no matter what happens to me or how far I roam.

A Place at the Table

I was looking through old photo albums last week and came upon some pictures of myself taken during the first years of my life along with those of family and friends during our many family dinners. These pictures reminded me of relatives and friends I had not thought about for a long time and made me cognizant of how quickly time passes, as here I am with grandchildren the age I was in the picture I was holding.

That picture was of the Sunday school class in 1955 when I was about four or five and my sister's friend, Agnes, was the Sunday school teacher. I loved her and listened attentively as she taught us the stories from the Bible that gave us the foundation upon which to build our budding faith.

I made a commitment to serve God at an altar call soon after my sixth birthday and have walked with God ever since, sometimes faithfully and sometimes not so faithfully. However, throughout my sixty-two years, I do not remember a time when I did not know God was present, even during the time of deep depression that followed the divorce from my first husband. When I have made that statement, some people have looked at me with consternation and asked, "How can you know God?" I replied with a like question, "How do you get to know anyone?"

The answer is really pretty simple: Spend some time with that person share a meal with them, and soon you will begin to understand their personality and their ways. Ask questions and soon their desires and wishes, kept close to their heart, will be revealed. This method is used in developing friendships and during courtship, so why not to develop a relationship with God? Simply ask Him to reveal Himself to you.

During the last two years, after a long period of self examination and reconciliation, I have been engaged in studies to become an assistant in my church. These studies have helped to deepen my relationship with God, and I have had some amazing encounters with Him that leave no doubt in my mind that He does exist and care for us. But I do understand that having an encounter with God seems like an impossible task when God is invisible and even an illusion to some people. So how do we begin to get to know a god who seems to be a figment of someone's imagination?

For me, the first step was to look at the world around me. My parents introduced me to the intricacies and details of nature, the order of all living things, and the seasonal functions of the universe when I was very young. We thanked God for His blessings at our table, examined the wonder of new birth of animals and plants in spring and watched the seasonal changes of growth and death throughout the year. Because of the wise tutelage of my parents I became convinced at a young age that this was all too complex to be an accident and is instead the plan of a Creator.

Some doubters have given disclaimers to the creation story, trying to convince the world that the universe happened by some fantastic accident or Big Bang. At this point, I am reminded of this joke:

> Two scientists came to God and said, "You see, God, we have figured out how life was formed, and so we can prove now that you did not create all living things."
>
> "Okay," God says. "Prove it to me. I'm listening."
>
> The first scientist picks up a handful of dirt and says, "First of all, you take some dirt and . . ."
>
> "Whoa!" says God. "You go make your own dirt!"

I know it is not that simple, but many of the world's most educated scientists have been baffled by the intricate functions of the universe and are unable to explain the functions and building blocks of nature without adding the term *intelligent design*. I believe this is another way of admitting that a creator does exist. If we think that God has stopped creating, I can assure you that the next time you see a newborn baby or a lamb or foal, you are seeing His creation still in progress. The new buds in spring after the long, cold winter are signs of His continued renewal of the creation he began so long ago.

Even after accepting that there is a creator, there is more. That "more" for me was a missing ingredient, an intrinsic place within me that needed filling. Some call it the God-shaped hole that can only be satisfied by knowing God, by filling it with a personal relationship with Him. Throughout history, people have tried to fill that hole with other things, such as possessions, activities, other relationships, drugs, or alcohol.

During my teen years, even though I had faith in God from a very early age, I put my relationships with friends and the young man whom I married at age eighteen before my relationship with God. I wondered why that marriage fell apart and did not really come to grips with the fact that it was an upside down relationship until years later. As so many others have done, I looked to my husband, whose love was at best a poor substitute for the love of God, to satisfy the longing for true love, joy, and peace.

After much soul searching, I came to a deeper understanding of God's proper place in my life and began to understand that only He could hold first place in my heart. I then understood why my divorce had happened and understood that God was trying to remold me into a humbler, more empathetic person by allowing me to suffer rejection and the loss of my pride. I had been living with such pride about the choices I had made, and I had not once consulted God about those choices. Yes, God does give us free will to choose our own way, but he is a jealous God and will not let us go easily. The first Commandment tells us that nothing and no one should be more important than our relationship with God.

Finally, I understood that God could use that most humbling event in my life if I would use the experience to empathize with and witness to other young, divorced women whom I encountered at work and socially. I could relate more fully to their pain and struggles. That realization made me a kinder, gentler manager at my new job and continues to, even now thirty years later, make me aware of the needs of this confused and hurting world.

My relationships with other people began to flourish and grow after I had returned to a right-side-up relationship with God. During those years of exile, while I shed many tears and did much self-examination, I found that God was always there for me in the form of a pastor and his wife who loved and helped me through my feelings of rejection and betrayal. I began to understand more fully how Christ must have felt when those around him betrayed and forsook Him at the cross. Then He provided love and forgiveness for me through the actions of family and friends who supported me and provided an anchor for me to hang onto while I struggled to rebuild my battered ship.

After several years, He restored love to me when I met a Christian man, Ralph, who had had a similar experience of love and loss. We established a home together, anchoring our two battered ships in the safe harbour of God's love, and although we still struggled with human issues, we strove to put God first in our marriage and business. We loved to entertain our family and friends and because we both loved good food we were a great team when preparing and serving meals of celebration at Christmas and other occasions. We often invited a stranger or a new acquaintance to share those meals with us. We made a commitment to always have a place at the table for the people God led into our lives.

Those to whom I have witnessed about that period in my life have protested, "But God is invisible! How can I have a relationship with an invisible God?" So I asked them, "Is He truly invisible, or is He just not what you expect?" If you're expecting the grandfather with the long, white beard, you may be disappointed. I ask you to look at your family members who display how wonderfully intricate family characteristics are, including those that make you, you, a beautiful and unique individual. You are a child of the Creator, and like any parent, God wants to be in a relationship with you. Let's go to the Bible, God's book, to find what God has to say about the subject.

People have asked, "If there truly is a god who is so powerful, why would He want a relationship with little, insignificant me?" I then ask them, "Do you like to visit or have dinner with your family?" God tells us in the Bible that we are his family, and He wants to be close to us. So you may now be asking, "How can we know that we are a part of God's family?"

Take a look in the mirror. Now look at your own family and study the characteristics that have been passed down through generations. You see, our genetics equip us to be who we are: baker, sailor, tinker, tailor, or candlestick maker. We inherit those characteristics that make up our personality and our talents. In my family, if you watch the three generations of men—grandfather, father, and son—walking side by side, there is no doubt they belong to the same family. Even their voices are so similar that one has to ask which one is speaking on the telephone. Recently, at a family dinner, my daughter commented, "Mom, you have become Grandma." To me, it was a redundant statement, considering that two grandchildren were born in close succession. She explained, "No! I mean you have become a mirror image of your mother! You sound like her and do things the same way she did."

Just as we know that genetics define our character and appearance that make us part of a particular human family, if we are a part of God's family, we must also have characteristics that define us as part of that family. The Bible, the story of God's interaction with humans, tells us that we are created "in his own image" (Genesis 1:26-27). If that is true, we are a part of His genetic family and only have to look at how wonderfully and fearfully we are made to appreciate what He is like. If we consider this, we can probably list many characteristics we posses that reflect God's attributes, such as creativity, compassion, forgiveness, fun-loving, gentleness, anger, and many more. In Psalm 139:14, King David recognizes this when he says, "I will praise you, God, for I am fearfully and wonderfully made. Marvelous are your works, that my soul knows right well." Our innermost being, our soul, is equipped by God to recognize Him as our Father and to be in a relationship with Him just as we recognize members of our own family by their physical appearance, talents, and personalities. Even the prayer Christ taught us in Matthew 6: 9 begins with "Our Father . . . . "

The Bible is the primary way we can come to know and understand God. If you have never read it, I suggest you begin reading it like a book of short stories much like this book. The stories are connected by history, as it is the story of God's interaction with mankind along with a smattering of poetry and songs. I know it is long, and reading it seems like a daunting task, but I suggest you get a modern translation and begin at the beginning, reading one story at a time. Soon you will see that God takes great interest in the lives and welfare of His people. You won't understand it all at first, but as you get into the stories, you will begin to understand that it is not just an old book but also a real and vital invitation for you to have a relationship with Him today. You may find it really interesting and learn something of history in the process.

God issues several invitations that many of the recorded incidents illustrate. One of the most famous is found in Revelations 3:20, where Christ says, "Behold, I stand at the door and knock. If you hear my voice and open the door, I will come in and dine with you and you with me." We have an illustration of this verse in stained glass over the communion altar at our tiny log church. It depicts the Lord waiting for us to open the door. He wants a place at your table just as surely as the other members of your family do.

137

Once we believe in Christ, God provides the Holy Spirit who comes into our life as a guide and mentor. Without the Holy Spirit's presence, I would never have survived these last few years with having to deal with life on my own once more after my second husband, Ralph, passed away suddenly in 1998.

If you surrender to Him, you too will begin to understand God and see how interested He is in your life. He will sustain you and help you to understand Him if you will only ask. In Colossians 3:10 we read, "Having put on the new self, which is being renewed in knowledge in the image of the Creator." This verse tells us that through belief in and surrender to Christ's invitation; we leave the old life behind and will be restored to the image of God so that He will dwell with us once more through the Holy Spirit. We can never conform ourselves to the image of God through our own efforts, and it is not enough to resemble Him through good deeds or simply reflect His nature. It is only by becoming a genuine child of God that we can fully enjoy that wonderful, loving relationship and a place at His table.

Ephesians 2:8 says, "For it is by grace you have been saved, through faith—and this not by works, so that no one can boast." This means, His love and salvation are free! A gift! So I ask you, "What have we got to lose by asking Him to come into our lives so that He can share a place at our table?"

I challenge you to set an extra place at your table and issue an invitation. You may be surprised at who turns up.

Kick a Tire for Literacy

My son was born in 1969, a beautiful, healthy boy with dark, curly hair and big brown eyes. He was the perfect child for a very young first-time mother, as he was good-natured, ate well, and learned quickly. He began walking between ten and eleven months and loved to play outside by the time he was two. I will always carry the picture of him playing in Grandmother's garden, sitting among the plants and singing contentedly as he built highways for his toy cars in the dirt.

He loved to cuddle, and we had great times together reading stories and colouring pictures. For all intents and purposes, he was normal and healthy, reaching all the milestones as expected. As he began to print letters when he was about five, I noticed that he often turned some the letters around so they were backward. I chalked this up to beginner's mistakes and difficulty with the mechanics of printing, so I would take his little hand in mine to show him the correct way.

But the problem continued into first grade, where the class was very large and the teacher had very little time for one-on-one instruction. Her report at midterm said he was a slow learner and easily distracted. That did not sound like my boy, but with some concern, I found after much work that he still turned his letters and numbers around.

His problems persisted into second grade, where he had an elderly teacher who had little to no patience and was very poor in dealing with his problems. Soon, he did not want to go to school, and I learned that the teacher was encouraging his classmates to tease him about his inability to read. At parent-teacher interviews, she said he was lazy and was the class troublemaker. Again, that did not sound at all like the boy I knew and loved because at home he was quick to do the chores I asked him to do. He had a gentle, sweet way about him and got on well when playing with all the other children on the block.

In third grade, he had a lucky break. His teacher was a young graduate from university with a genuine desire to see her students succeed. About one month into the school year, I received an invitation to her class for an afternoon and saw for myself how my son was struggling with basic reading. After class, she told me she believed my son suffered from dyslexia, a condition she didn't know much about, but that he displayed the symptoms that were consistent with what she had learned so far. His inability to print letters correctly and poor reading skills were consistent with the textbook description of dyslexia.

By this time, he was able to communicate with us about the problems he was having. He told us the letters looked like little black bugs crawling across the page and that he couldn't make them stand still. That wonderful, young teacher made two suggestions. First, we were to have his eyes examined, and second, he was to go to a school called the Learning Assistance Centre, where specially trained teachers would do an assessment and work with him one-on-one.

Her diagnosis was confirmed, and a lifelong process of assisted learning began. We learned that he had no comprehension problems and in fact tested above average in that area. In some of the later grades, he was allowed to take oral tests because he knew his work but just had difficulty with reading and writing.

There were no teachers trained to cope with this disability at that time and very little funding for programs that would assist him. I fought many battles to keep him in mainstream education when the teachers and principals were ready to shuffle him aside into a vocational school. We spent many hours glued at the hip throughout his school years as I helped him to read instructions for homework, textbooks, and later

Shakespeare. It took time and patience, but he graduated from twelfth grade.

Today, he is a Registered Massage Therapist, a course which he passed with flying colours, his marks in the nineties. He assists me in running our dry cleaning plant, where he is a respected member of the community and is a wonderful father to two children. However, he still bears the emotional scars of his battle with this disability and has suffered from depression and often has low self-esteem because of it.

I hope that sharing my son's story will encourage anyone else who has this problem and they will come to know that they are not alone in the struggle and will take heart. The struggle is worth it, and you can overcome! You too can succeed! I also tell this story as a way of introducing you to one of Canada's everyday heroes, Peter Gzowski.

I was one of Peter Gzowski's greatest fans in the 1970s and '80s. I tried to listen every morning to the programs *This Country in The Morning* and then *Morning Side* that he hosted on CBC Radio every weekday. Regardless of where I was or what I was doing, the sound his voice carried me through the hour he was on. He interviewed the most interesting people and had a unique way of drawing people out to reveal a perspective that made one think deeply about the subjects. He opened his program, saying, "Good morning. I'm Peter Gzowski, and this is *Morning Side*" in that gruff, gravelly voice. I could see him sitting there at the microphone, a cup of coffee steaming nearby, as he prepared to reveal some interesting fact or personality. He was always dressed comfortably in baggy cords and a sweatshirt or sweater. His style of dress combined with his salt-and-pepper beard and mustache reminded me of a salty, wise, old sea captain who had come ashore from some distant and interesting land in order to enlighten us less informed landlubbers.

From Peter's vast experience as a journalist and editor of magazines or perhaps from the many people he interviewed, he became aware of the extreme need for literacy programs across the country. He felt it was a crime that so many could not read for one reason or another in this great, rich nation of Canada. For those of us who had struggled to find programs for our children, and for the adults who had slipped through the cracks and had never learned to read in the education system, this became a beacon of hope.

There was never enough money to fund the necessary special education programs, so Peter became determined to do something about this. His mantra became; we must give everyone a fair chance in the world by giving them the opportunity to learn to read and so he set out to raise awareness about the problems facing the illiterate and set about raising funds for local schools and programs. Thus began the Peter Gzowski Invitational Golf Tournament for Literacy in 1986. It took three years to build momentum until there were tournaments from coast to coast, but what better way than a golf game to rally the literate, well-heeled celebrities of society to assist in the cause?

In 1989, I worked for a lovely couple who owned a dry cleaning plant in Calgary who were always very concerned about their employees' lives and tried to support us wherever they could. That was the same year my son was graduating from high school and considering the difficulties he had encountered along the way, this was cause for much celebration. One day we heard CBC Radio announce that Peter Gzowski, my hero, was coming to Calgary to host a golf tournament for literacy that fall, they knew I would be interested. When they offered to pay the fees for me to attend and further more offered to make a donation in my son's name, I was overjoyed and humbled at the opportunity! But in the next breath, I lamented that I had never learned to golf and had never even been on a course. They then hired a golf pro to give me a quick set of lessons, and I went out to purchase a set of golf clubs.

The tournament was a Texas Scramble and would Tee off at eight AM, rain or shine. I awoke early, so excited to get on this great adventure, and found to my dismay, upon looking out the window that a new, eight-inch blanket of snow covered all of Calgary. I phoned the golf course and was assured the tournament would still continue. So off I went to Willow Park Golf and Country Club, where we were treated to a hot breakfast and introduced to our host, Peter. There were plenty of jokes about the "warm? welcome" we offered him. Then we were divided into teams, handed orange balls so we could find them in the snow, and we were off to golf for a good cause.

By the time we reached our tee the day had warmed up considerably, as September days in southern Alberta are known to do, and the snow had reached a consistency perfect for making snowballs and snowmen. This added to the challenge of the game because with each step, the tires of our golf cart collected the sticky snow and grew in size until we looked like we were dragging large oddly shaped snowmen. Soon, the carts were so heavy we couldn't pull them and we had to stop often to bang the wheels to knock off the snow.

Our team, comprised of three men and myself, was in fine humour and determined to make the most of the day, despite the added challenge of the weather. We soon developed a method of keeping the tires clear of snow as we went down the fairway from one hole to the next. We formed a conga line, following each other single file, singing the conga song: bum pa bum pa bum . . . bum—kick. The singing kept us moving along in good spirits, and the kick freed the tires of our golf carts of snow. Soon we were laughing so hard it was hard to take a serious swing at our orange balls as they plopped into one snow bank after the other. The fairway soon looked like it had been invaded by a colony of very large gophers because we had to find and dig the balls out of the snowdrifts after each shot.

The day turned out to be really fun despite the added challenge of the snowman who had dumped on us. Evening found everyone coming back to the nineteenth hole in high good humour. We met many of Calgary's celebrities during cocktails and listened to an inspiring speech from Peter. I had the privilege of having dinner with people from *The Herald* and Lanny MacDonald, who was playing for the Calgary Flames at that time. The highlight for me, however, was the few minutes I got to say thank you to Peter in person for his efforts on behalf of the illiterate. He gave me his full attention as I told him about my son, which was the reason I was there, and he in turn told me it was stories like mine that made what he did worthwhile.

I appreciate that the PGI Tournament continues to earn millions of dollars for people to achieve reading skills they might not have otherwise. However, some young people golfing in those tournaments today don't know much if anything about Peter Gzowski, the man. But this grandmother, who golfed in the first PGI Tournament in Calgary, still remembers what a privilege it was to kick a tire for literacy with Peter and the other fine folk from our community. I want to pay tribute to the caring man Peter was and to his dream of giving every person the gift of a chance to read. It has been said that Peter is credited with making Canadians aware of the soul of this country.

I am aware that Peter struggled with many personal issues before his death in 2002, but I feel this verse from Proverbs 12:14 is an appropriate tribute to this man who was a gifted radio journalist and a caring philanthropist: "From the fruit of his lips a man is filled with good things as surely as the work of his hands rewards him." Peter's words of encouragement to those who believe in his cause, echo in our minds every time we participate in another Peter Gzowski Golf Tournament. However, it is the students who are learning to read who receive the rewards.

Oh, My Papa

Several years ago, I had the privilege to meet and get to know a family of Italian descent who were clients of the dry cleaning business I was managing. During the eight years I lived and worked in that community, I met many families, but the Esposito's were and remain special to me to this day.

Mr. Esposito, Vincenzo, or Papa Vinnie as everyone called him, was one of those men who was larger than life. I know that sounds trite, but he really was. He was distinguished as Italian men often are, sporting rugged good looks and a wavy shock of salt-and-pepper hair. He was broader and taller than most Italian man of his generation, as most had been deprived of good food during the Second World War. He said he owed this to his father, who had taken them to live in peace out in the hill country with an aunt, where good food could still be had while the war was raging around them. He had a big, booming voice that carried for a city block and used it to sing at the top of his lungs for his family and anyone else who was in the vicinity. He was a hale and hearty man who was always in good spirits.

Mr. Esposito's wife, Lena, was a beautiful lady when she was younger, and that beauty had been refined into a kind of regal grace by hard work, childbearing, and the passing years. They ran an Italian restaurant together, where both put their heart and soul into serving their clientele. They had three children, a beautiful and talented girl named Maria and two boys, Vinnie Jr. and Marco, who was the clown of the family. The whole family dealt with me for years, and their jovial way lifted my spirits when they picked up their clean clothing or brought in a pasta-and-wine-stained tablecloth after the latest family meal.

We became friendly as the years passed, and I received many invitations to their home for summer barbecues and celebratory dinners marking a family member's birthday, anniversary, or christening. They celebrated life in their lovely home and huge, pie-shaped backyard that was filled with vegetables, flowerbeds, and a comfortable patio. The welcome mat was always out, and people dropped in for a drink or a meal without an invitation. Someone was always cooking and people felt at ease because of the hearty welcome. The little children ran and played among the adults and were hardly ever reprimanded for their boisterous behaviour unless they were fighting. You could feel the love that bound this family together and sustained them through the years of hard work and even harder play.

During those visits, I came to know Papa Vinnie for all that he was to his family and the community he served. He was a cherished husband to his wife, who worshipped him and was never far from his side. He was the beloved patriarch to his own children and many others from the community to whom he gave love, advice, and reprimands in equal measure. He was the driving force of their business and any other endeavour that he put his hand to. He was a pillar of the community, setting the standard high because he was always the first to volunteer for the school fundraiser, coaching the soccer team, or flipping pancakes for the annual Shrove Tuesday supper at the church. He served with humility at the church and was a jovial role model in the community hall. You could always hear him before you saw him, and you just knew the event was going to go better because Vinnie and Lena were there. Lena and his children were always first in his life next to God, whom he worshipped with the true faith of one who had a personal and intimate relationship with his Lord.

One day late in January, Lena came in to pick up the cleaning, and I could tell she was not her usual self. She was pale, and I saw she had been crying. With the ease that comes from many years of friendship, I enquired if she was feeling okay. "I'm okay. It'sa notta me. It'sa Papa Vinnie," she wailed, bursting into tears again. "He'sa not feel so good for a while now. So last week, I make him go to the doctor. Today, the doctor calls us both to come. He tells us Vinny, he has the cancer." She could hardly choke out the words, and her shoulders shook with sobs that wracked her slender frame. I sat with her then, giving her a cup of tea and tried to encourage her by telling her that treating cancer had become much more successful in recent years. I also reminded her that Vinnie was going to need her to be strong now, and that he was going to need everyone to be positive to help him fight this terrible disease. After a time, her crying eased, and she put on the stoic mask that remained on her face for the next year.

It was a difficult year for the Esposito family. Vinnie Jr. became more active in the business and the many roles his father held in the community. He tried so hard to fill those shoes, but we all could see that the shoes were still a little too big, and he was struggling. He went forward, putting on a brave face with the rest of the family following his example. Every time I saw one of them, I would ask about Papa, and the answer was usually the same, "He's hangin' in!" the younger set said, but Lena's eyes spoke volumes as they filled up and she asked us to pray.

Pray we did, but as the year drew to a close, they admitted that Papa Vinnie was losing the battle, and a pall of grief settled on the faces of his family and friends. I had been to visit once or twice early on, but when I went the final time just before Christmas, I was appalled at the toll this disease had taken on this once vibrant man. He was shrunken and diminished both in stature and strength. Only his eyes held their former fervour as he squeezed my hand with a grip still as strong as steel, while he said in a voice barely audible, "Thank you for your prayers, my friend! I'll see you on the other side!"

I was present at the funeral, a Catholic high mass. The church was bursting at the seams with people of many walks and faiths. So many, in fact, that they filled the church and spilled out into the parking lot where speakers broadcast the service into the cold winter air. The final Scripture reading was one that Vinnie had chosen himself from 2 Timothy 4:1-8:

> In the presence of God and of Christ Jesus, who will judge the living and the dead, and in view of his appearing and his kingdom, I give you this charge: Preach the Word; be prepared in season and out of season; correct, rebuke, and encourage—with great patience and careful instruction. For the time will come when men will not put up with sound doctrine. For the time will come when they will gather around them a great number of teachers to say what their itching ears want to hear. They will turn their ears away from the truth and turn aside to myths. But you, keep your head in all situations, endure hardship, do the work of an evangelist, discharge all duties of your ministry.
>
> For I am already being poured out like a drink offering, and the time has come for my departure. I have fought the good fight, I have finished the race, I have kept the faith. Now there is in store for me the crown of righteousness, which the Lord, the righteous Judge, will award to me on that day—and not only to me, but also to all who have believed and longed for his appearing.

Grown men cried unabashedly that day as they bid farewell to one of the best friends they had ever known.

About a week later, Vinnie Jr. dropped by to bring in the clothing they had worn for the funeral, and again I asked how everyone was doing. He said they were slowly coming to accept that Papa Vinnie was gone, but it was going to be hard adjusting to the empty place in their home. Then he said he had to run because he was on his way to the bank with the family. He explained that when they had read Papa's will, he had requested that the whole family be present when they opened his safe deposit box because it contained a great treasure. Vinnie Jr. was puzzled because his father had handed over all the records of the company, and although they were comfortable, he didn't think there had ever been enough money to sock away any great treasure.

When he came back to pick up the clean clothing, he was beaming. He told me that in the safe deposit box (one of the largest, by the way) was a parcel for each child and grandchild. When they unwrapped them, they found all the things they had made for Papa Vinnie when they were little children: the crooked clay ash trays, the lumpy frogs, and faded Christmas decorations, as well as the cards each had 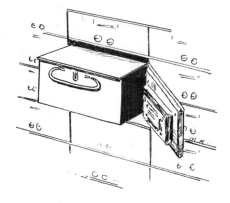 made for Father's Days and Christmases past and some of their better pieces of artwork. Each parcel also contained a picture of that child with Papa Vinnie, just the two of them, sitting some place side-by-side reading a book, roasting a hot dog, or petting the dog, commemorating the time they had shared. There was a letter too, which caused Vinnie Jr. and me to shed tears when he read it to me. Basically, the letter told them that silver and gold were useless unless you had a family to share it with, and that his family was "his greatest treasure."

This is a true story; however, with their permission the names have been changed to guard the privacy of the family.

Don't Worry! Have Faith!

We have all heard the song "Don't Worry, Be Happy" on the radio and have enjoyed the message and the funky reggae beat. But if we truly think about the song's message, it is comparable to Christ's message when He told us not to worry.

I recently drove by a church that has a billboard out front on which is posted messages, quips, and quotes. On this particular day, the message posted was "Worry Ends Where Faith Begins." Parked beside the sign, as if an exclamation point for the message was a brand-spanking-new SUV with its front grill and hood badly smashed in. Under the front stood a rubber tote to catch the coolant draining from the damaged radiator.

If you have ever been involved in an accident, you know that it is hard—in fact, impossible—to not worry about what will happen next. I recalled the distress I felt when in an accident and now felt that same distress for the driver who had caused this accident, which perhaps was the person driving the SUV, not to mention the driver of the other vehicle with whom the collision had occurred. They would have had to decide whose fault the accident was and the insurance implications. The police probably charged the person who caused the accident, and there were probably fines as well if a traffic violation had occurred. They would have had to find out where to take the vehicles for repair and arrange for transportation for the

150

period of time it would take for those repairs. An accident of this severity could also have caused injuries, such as whiplash or spinal distress, which could take months and even years of therapy to heal. I have seen someone rendered unable to work because of injuries from such an accident, and it is hard to imagine anyone going through such an experience without some mental distress and possibly even depression. Yet here was this sign with its bold message firmly planted in biblical truth, encouraging us to not worry but simply have faith. At this point, we could quote the verse from Romans 8:28. "And we know that in all things God works for the good of those who love Him." But it might be hard to believe when looking at that damaged car.

Often our reluctance to surrender our everyday experiences to God is what causes us the most grief. Yes, I mean everything from the car accident, the problems we are having at work or in our relationships right down to the tiniest details of our lives like what to wear for a special dinner. Does Christ not tell us in Matthew 6: 25:

> Therefore I tell you do not worry about your life, what you will eat or drink; or about your body, what you will wear. Is life not more important than food and the body more important than clothes? Look at the birds of the air; they do not sow or reap or store away in barns, and yet your heavenly Father feeds them. Are you not much more valuable than they? Who of you by worrying can add a single hour to his life?

So Christ rebukes us for worrying about these everyday things and challenges us to have faith that He will provide later in verse 30, saying: "Oh, you of little faith. So do not worry, saying, 'What shall we eat?' or 'What shall we drink?' or 'What shall we wear?' For the pagans run after these things, and your heavenly Father knows that you have need of them." Then the final challenge is given in verse 33:

> But seek ye first the kingdom of God, his kingdom, and his righteousness and all these things will be given to you as well. Therefore do not worry about tomorrow, for tomorrow will worry about itself. Each day has enough trouble of its own.

It is the ultimate test of our faith to rest assured that God knows what we need and will supply our needs. In Philippians 4:4-7, Paul writes,

> Rejoice in the Lord always, and again I say, Rejoice! Let your gentleness be evident to all. The Lord is near. Do not be anxious for anything, but in everything, by prayer and supplication, with thanksgiving, present your requests to God, and he shall supply all your needs according to his riches in glory.

Yes, He will even help us when we have a car accident!

In that same chapter of Philippians, I found my grandmother's favourite verse, which summed up her faith:

> I know what it is to be in need, and I know what it is to have plenty. I have learned the secret of being content in any and every situation, whether well fed or hungry, whether living in plenty or in want. I can do everything through Him who gives me strength! (Philippians 4:12).

Are we truly ready to relinquish control of the details of our lives and place them in God's hands? If we are truly committed to Christ, we can rest assured in the promises made in Romans 8:28.

I encourage you to read the rest of Romans 8 and consider its implications for you and your life. Oh, and by the way, I pray you will have safe travels!

Good Ol' Boys

In every rural neighborhood, there are men who are referred to as good ol' boys. Some would say it is a derogatory term, but I believe they are called this because they are literally good and dependable for all sorts of service they provide to the community.

Today at the intersection of two major country roads, there was an impromptu convention being held. Three trucks were parked at the intersection with four men I recognized sitting on fenders and leaning against truck boxes, their battered  caps pushed back on their heads. They were chewing on straws taken from one of the bales that one of these good ol' boys was hauling. By all appearances, they were having a serious conversation about various topics, perhaps politics, the price of gasoline, politics, the price of feed, politics, the price of cows, and who would win the Stanley Cup. They might have been making plans to help at the local rodeo or the town parade. Maybe they were discussing their wives' latest hobby (probably shopping), how their kids were doin' in school, and whether that other neighbor up the way needed help finishing the fence around his calf pasture now that he had broken his leg.

You see, I have been privy to these conversations when I tagged along with my father or brother when I was a kid, and I know how important these men are to the people who live in the area. During such conversations, a general feeling of solidarity and community is established and the backbone of that community becomes a little stronger. The male bonding that occurs over the truck box establishes how that area will survive and even thrive in spite of fires, floods, economic recession, or the political mayhem of the nation.

So coming upon this scene today made me smile for the whole day. You see, I've seen those same men come to the aid of the local women's organization, setting up tables and flippin' flapjacks or grillin' hot dogs to raise funds for the local church. I've seen them rounding up cattle together and making short work of that fence for that injured neighbor. I've seen them come to the preschool with a couple of newborn calves or a puppy for the class to pet. I've seen them cheering for the home team at the baseball diamond, local curling rink, or simply doin' up skates and coachin' the youngsters hockey team. I've seen them just leaning against the boards, visiting with their neighbors while the kids skate on a Friday night. I've also seen them work shoulder-to-shoulder settin' up chairs for the kids' Christmas concert or heftin' sandbags when the local creek swells over its banks in spring to threaten their little town. I've seen them in good-natured fun at the local fair, competing in the wild cow milking contest or horse race. And I've seen them deadly serious, lecturing their kids about their behaviour. I've seen them all gussied up for a Saturday night dance or a wedding, and I've seen them standing with solemn grief on those weathered faces, hat in hand, as they bid farewell to a friend or relative at a funeral.

These men, young and old, who can be found meeting at the side of the road or in the local coffee shop for lunch or working together at some community event, are the backbone of rural society. They support families and local enterprise. They make our country richer by their hard work but also because they display the true values stable families and strong communities are built upon. As I watched them there by the side of the road, I was reminded of this passage from Proverbs 27:17-19, 21:

> As iron sharpens iron, so one man sharpens another.
> He who tends a fig tree will eat of its fruit
> And he who looks after his Master will be honoured.
> As water reflects a face, so a man's heart reflects the man.
> The crucible for silver and the furnace for gold,
> But man is tested by the praise he receives.

Happy Father's Day to each one of you Good ol' Boys!

The Queen of the Corner

On a fine spring evening, I was making my way home after an hour or two of shopping. The air was warm, and the stars were just becoming visible through the golden glow from the city lights. As I approached the corner of Southland Crossing, the traffic light turned red. Since this is the intersection of two main streets, this corner has a rather long light, so I relaxed, tapping a beat on the steering wheel in time with the music on my radio.

It was then that I became aware of the striking young lady who stood beside a shopping cart next to the curb, also waiting for the light to change. She was tall with smooth skin the colour of ebony. Her tightly curled hair was caught up in a rather ornate hair clip, and she swayed with a rhythm all her own. I noticed that she had begun to sing, so I quickly turned off the radio and rolled down my window so that I might eavesdrop.

The sound of her rich contralto voice resonated through the evening air, and I caught the words and melody of an old hymn that I had learned in childhood. "Oh when the roll is called up yonder, when the roll is called up yonder, I'll be there!" She sang the hymn with reverence but served it up on the cadence of a reggae beat. I sat spellbound for a minute, held so by her presence and her singing. When the light turned green, she stooped with regal dignity, reached

into the cart to pick up her scepter, a common corn broom wrapped in the Canadian Tire bag with our country's emblem, the Maple Leaf, emblazoned on it, and a golden melon, which she carried on the palm of her left hand in the same fashion as the Queen of England carries her golden orb.

By chance, mine was the only vehicle at the light, so I hesitated my departure when the light turned green in order to observe this Queen of Southland Crossing, for I could think of her as nothing less as I observed the regal bearing with which she carried herself and her wares.

I could still hear her flamboyantly singing with assurance, the anthem of the kingdom she anticipated as she turned toward the apartment building, which I'm sure was her castle. Though I know not her name nor from whence she came, this noble Queen of the Corner delivered her testimony of joy and hope, unaware that I, her humble subject, had been allowed this brief audience and will be forever changed.

My heart is steadfast, O God; I will sing and make music with all my soul. Awake, harp and lyre!

I will awaken the dawn. I will praise you, O Lord, among the nations; I will sing of you among the peoples. For great is your love, higher than the heavens; Your faithfulness reaches the skies.

Be exalted, O God, above the heavens, and let your glory be over all the earth (Psalm 108:1-5).

Signs of Our Lives

The sign that hangs beside my front door proclaims, "WELCOME TO GRANDMA'S HOUSE!" and has three small hearts hanging from it that read: "Kids Spoiled Here!" "Open 24 Hours!" "Free Cookies and Kisses!"

I love those kitschy signs that have cute sayings and sometimes great truths or intelligent quotes printed on them and have to limit how many I buy. For instance, inside my kitchen, there is one a friend gave to me, a painted wooden wreath with a heart hanging inside that says, "Home is where you hang your heart." Another sign offers "Free Hugs. One size fits all."

In the laundry room, there is a painted washboard that says, "Cleanliness is next to Godliness." The washboard and the saying were both favourites of my mother and they, along with the skills she taught me, remind me of the love and care she put into washing, mending, and ironing our clothing.

On my mantle are two words wrought in antiqued gold letters: *Faith* and *Peace*, the two blessings I hope to impart to each and every guest when they come to visit. Another word on the dining room china cupboard is *Laugh*, and since laughter is touted as the best medicine along with good food and friendship, I hope it encourages lighthearted and jolly conversation at my table.

Next to an antique writing desk that I use to display pictures of friends and family, I have a card that reads, "The best antiques are old friends." It reminds me to drop a note or send an e-mail to people I haven't seen recently.

In the hall is a picture of me surrounded by children, sharing a story with my granddaughter's class. The frame has this verse printed on it, "A hundred years from now, it will not matter what my bank account was, the sort of house I lived in, or the kind of car I drove, but the world may be different because I was important in the life of a child!" When I look at it, I am reminded that it is not those words or even the truth they convey that is important but rather the time spent with and teaching those small children that has effected change in their lives and mine.

So many of us have quotes from famous people hanging around. I found a sampler by General Grant's wife, Lizzy, in 1852 with a quotation from the Proverbs 24: 3 that says, "By wisdom a house is built and by understanding it is established, by knowledge the rooms are filled with all precious and pleasant riches."

That got me to thinking about the collections I have accumulated over years of travelling. After several years of marriage, my husband finally understood that the souvenirs I brought back from holiday were visual reminders of the love we shared and of the time we spent together rather than being mere trinkets and dust collectors, which is what he called them. Some years ago, I found a verse that had been carefully framed and dated 1929 that has become my mantra:

A little more kindness, a little less speed.
A little more giving, a little less greed.
A little more smile, a little less frown.
A little less kicking a man when he's down.
Share a few more flowers as we pass through strife.
And put fewer on graves at the end of life!

We may read books that are classics, such as the Bible, Shakespeare, or Henry David Thoreau, and quote words that impart to us the very foundation of our society, but *if we do not live every day the truths* of love, hope, and charity that we learn from those great works, *we are as useless as a soundless bell* and may as well spend our time doing something other than reading.

We put up signs that impart the rules of the road or others that give directions to places of importance, but if we don't act upon their directions or reminders, we are sure to go the wrong way. We can put up signs in our houses about what we believe, but if we don't practice what they say, they become a mockery of us all. We may just as well hang up a pretty picture instead.

"What good is it, my brothers, if a man claims to have faith but no deeds? You see a person is justified by what he does and not by faith alone. As the body without the spirit is dead, so faith without deeds is dead" (James 2:14, 24, 26).

Waltzing With a Paper Bag

It was the Saturday of Thanksgiving weekend, and I had been shopping for the groceries for the traditional dinner: turkey, yams, cranberries, and more. I had also picked up some cheap, day-old bread to make dressing. The young man at the store carefully packed the four loaves standing on end in a brown paper bag.

When I arrived home, I unpacked the groceries and stored the meat, vegetables, and frozen food first. By the time I got to the four loaves of bread, it was time to cut them up into cubes for the dressing. I took each from the bag, making short work of dicing them as I went. We love dressing in our house, so I usually double the recipe that was handed down from my mother. When I finished dicing, I added sage, parsley, and other savoury herbs to the bread crumbs. My hands were busy with the food, so I did not stop to fold up the bag, which I had pushed aside near the garbage can.

When I finished the prep work for the dressing, my next task was making the pumpkin pies. I could have purchased a couple at the store, but my granddaughter said she was looking forward to my homemade pies, so here I was at seven p.m. just beginning to mix the spicy filling. As I rushed back and forth between the cupboard and the fridge for eggs, cream, and spices, it seemed that the bag took on a life of its own. Every time I turned from the mixing bowl, it was there in front of me again, just begging to be filled, and every time, I pushed it back beside the garbage can with my foot, leaving it empty.

I don't know how or why, but the bag kept moving back into my path while I was running back and forth from the fridge to the counter. Maybe the draft from the open window was pushing it along the kitchen floor, or perhaps there was just enough movement generated by the air currents set in motion as the grandchildren chased each other around the island. For whatever reason, the bag continued to migrate out of its place next to the garbage can to the middle of the floor in front of me, and I continued to waltz with it for the next half hour, determined to finish the pies before I undertook the task of tidying the kitchen.

I was making three pies, and the recipe for the filling called for six eggs. As I began to crack them into a bowl, the bag sidled up to my leg, just begging me to toss the shells into it, which suddenly seemed the most logical thing to do. I tossed eggshells, veggie peels, and all things compostable into it. And of course the bag was compostable paper too, so it could be put into the composter as well. How perfect! Feeling like Susie Homemaker and relieved that the bag had found a purpose other than just trying to be my dancing partner, I continued to work happily.

Now that it was firmly anchored to its spot by the weight of the eggshells and a few scraps from our late dinner, the bag no longer danced across the floor from the space beside the garbage can. I finished the pies with relief and retired to the library to prepare for the Sunday morning communion service with which I had been asked to assist. Then I went to prepare for bed in peace, never giving my friend, the bag, another thought.

I woke the next morning at my usual time of six-thirty and went to the kitchen to make coffee. I dumped the previous days coffee grounds into the bag and happily began chopping celery and onions to add to the bread for dressing I would use to stuff the turkey. All those bits went into the bag, joining the eggshells, supper scraps, and coffee grounds for the composter. By the time I had prepared the salad, peeled potatoes and sweet potatoes, and cleaned the broccoli, the bag was more than half full.

It was soon time to leave for church. I looked at the clock, proud of my organizational skills that allowed me to be ahead of schedule. I had just enough time to give the kitchen floor a lick and a promise so it would shine for our company. I gathered up the bits and pieces that had made their way onto the floor and attempted to carry the handy recyclable bag and its contents out to the composter.

The bag had been sitting in its spot beside the garbage can with all that kitchen waste in it for about twelve hours, looking so innocent and fulfilled. But little did I know it was just biding its time to take revenge on me for not recognizing its true worth as *a beautiful dancing partner*. Soon it would reveal its shortcomings as a compost receptacle. And what sweet revenge it had!

As I lifted the bag, the bottom, which last night had slid its way across the kitchen floor with such ease and grace, gave way with a sickening, sucking, ripping noise, depositing its entire contents all over the newly washed floor and my feet. I groaned, realizing that my choice to use this *ugly* brown paper bag as a compost bag had just cost me my bit of spare time as well as my Susie Homemaker pride.

After cleaning all that yuck (my grandson's comment) from the floor and rewashing the tile and my feet, I rushed off to church in a flap with hardly a minute to spare. And what do you think I saw on the church bulletin board as I came in? Some loving church member had placed this clipping that read, "The only thing that cannot be recycled is wasted time." *Ha, Ha! Very funny!* I thought as I rushed to help with the service. *Would I love to have a word or two with that individual!*

So I urge you to be aware of your choices, for every choice you make *will* come back to help or hinder you sometime in the future. Coincidentally, one of the Bible passages for the day was from Proverbs 16:2-3: "All a man's ways seem innocent to him, but motives are weighed by the Lord. Commit to the Lord whatever you do, and your plan will succeed."

A Bird in the Planter is Worth . . . ?

In late November 2010, I filled the two big pots on my front step with spruce boughs, pine branches, and sprays of juniper and holly berries. They were so beautiful, and I didn't want them to die too soon, so I asked a florist friend of mine how I could make those fantastic displays last into January. She suggested I fill the pots with water and allow it to freeze, as this would seal off the stems to prevent moisture loss on the cold, dry days and allow them to drink a little if we had a Chinook, that warm wind Alberta is famous for in winter. What my friend didn't know then was that this would be one of the most steadily cold winters we have had in the last ten years. So here we are on the fifteenth day of March 2011, without having had a Chinook to warm us above freezing until *finally* today the temperature has reached hesitantly above zero.

My beloved pots of greenery long ago turned from lively, proud green displays of welcome to sad, brown, droopy leftover remnants of a season past. I would really love to be rid of them! However, because they are quite large and still filled with that big block of ice, which has not once melted

enough to drain them, they sit on the step like a pair of ancient sentinels, guarding a season they will not let us forget.

Today when I came home after delivering the grandchildren to school, in the dried-up branches and berries was a whole flock of chickadees scavenging for the pine seeds and bugs still available.

Although the greenery is a sorry sight indeed and no longer useful for the purpose it was intended, it has provided a useful source of energy for the birds. I sat in the car and watched the birds' activities as they fluttered and pecked among the cones and dried berries. They called to each other and soon more joined them as they shared the bounty they had found.

The flock and its camaraderie reminded me of the ladies who are members of Soroptimist International, an organization to which I belong. Our members are mostly older women with children who have grown and fledged. There are a few younger women who have joined us and are learning the ropes of fundraising and volunteering. We meet on Tuesday evenings in a beautiful, old sandstone building that was once used as a school. Although formerly beaten and battered from hard use by the students, the McDougal Centre has been polished and restored so that now it is repurposed as a convenient meeting place for clubs like ours and for the provincial government when it is important for it to visit the south end of the province.

If you watched us as the ladies meet, you would see that we flutter and chirp around the lovely plates of treats that some members provide before our meetings. We share food and information. We encourage each other in our personal endeavours and generally have fun as we congregate in this once dejected building. Among the older members, there are teachers and business and professional women who have many useful insights from their lives to share. Although many are still actively working, some are in various stages of retirement from their chosen careers. Instead of becoming fruitless, depressed, and a drain on society, these women have found new purpose in their volunteer work and from the friendship they find at the meetings in this now beautifully restored and repurposed old building. Just as the birds found new purpose and became revitalized with energy while sharing food and camaraderie in the pots of dried evergreens, these women also leave their meetings with renewed vitality and intentions.

They offer mentoring and support to various charitable organizations with their knowledge, time, and funding. I have had times when I felt like I was getting old and was no longer useful to my family or community, but becoming active in this way has restored my vigour and drive.

The flock of chickadees flew off suddenly en masse as if by some inaudible signal to find some other activity, and I went into the house with insight and a quiet, inner joy gained from watching them. They had found new energy from the food they gleaned among my ancient, dried-up pine boughs. I poured a cup of coffee and thought, *Fly on! Fly high, my fine, feathered friends! You are just like our ladies club with seeds of knowledge to share and places to go to keep you active. Who knows what heights your inspiration and example can encourage others to achieve?*

I sat down that morning for my devotional time which included these verses from Hebrews 6:10-12:

> God is not unjust; he will not forget your work and the love you have shown Him as you have helped His people and continue to help them. We want each of you to show this same diligence to the very end, in order to make our *hope* sure. We do not want you to become lazy, but to imitate those who through faith and patience inherit what has been promised.

I had to ask, what is my hope? I hope that each person I come in contact with might come to know Christ's love as a result of the care and patient help they receive from me as I volunteer!

A Wake-Up Call

We don't like to use pesticides or herbicides on our little acreage, as we have too much to lose by spraying them around. Most important, I have two *beautiful* grandchildren who are exposed to enough pollution in this world without having these chemicals in their own yard.

Then there is the little dog, Missy, who loves to ramble out on the grass, sniffing at the various mole holes and mouse trails. When she comes in, she often cleans her feet by licking them like a cat, so it would not be kind to expose her to those chemicals. Then, of course, we want the bumblebees and honeybees to survive so they can make their way to our garden and flowerbeds to pollinate our crops. Last week, during an especially warm spell, we had a hatch of butterflies in the yard. The children came in to play the CD *Bullfrogs and Butterflies: They've Both Been Born Again* after we had identified at least three or four varieties. I'm sure those lovely creatures would not have survived if we had sprayed any pesticides.

A neighbor who was admiring the butterflies asked how we kept all the so-called bad insects and weeds under control. I told her the answer is really quite simple: you pull up or dig out the weeds and encourage birds to come and stay by putting up bird houses and feeding stations, then they will catch and feed the insects to their young,. Did you know that one pair of robins hatching four chicks will catch approximately four liters of bugs in order to feed their babies from the time they hatch until they are ready to leave the nest? Swallows will keep the mosquito population under control, and house wrens have a similar history. Chickadees and other tree-loving birds can be seen hanging upside down, cleaning bug infestations from the tree branches. Wood peckers will drill for unseen pests that can kill your trees. It is so easy to encourage nature to look after itself by leaving some natural habitat undisturbed. Putting up a few nesting boxes or bird feeders and leaving some natural areas untouched encourages animals and birds to find our property attractive and therefore benefits us as well.

I wrote the above article for a local paper after the neighbors visit and listening to a radio broadcast lamenting the demise of the prairie songbirds, grouse and burrowing owls. Am I overly simplistic in my belief that we need to share the planet, and that God designed it to look after its self and we humans as well if we could just learn not to disturb the balance of nature?

Disturb. Now there is an interesting word!

On a lovely spring Sunday morning, I realized I didn't have to get up to go to work and was about to turn over for another half hour of snooze time, when there was an extremely loud *rat-a-tat-tat* coming from somewhere in the house. I sat bolt upright, all thoughts of sleep having fled. It sounded like machine gun fire or a motor in rapid backfire. At first, I thought it might be our well pump in the process of blowing a piston.

I hurriedly grabbed a robe and ran out of my bedroom to investigate and ran into my son, clutching his robe around him, saying, "What in the world?!"

We were both baffled by the extremely loud staccato noise. Just then, it repeated. We looked at each other and then at the fireplace, as the sound seemed to be emanating from there. The firebox amplified the ricocheting noise around the living room and through the Sunday-morning stillness of the house.

"Something is in the chimney!" I exclaimed.

"Ya think?" was my son's rude reply as he opened the door to the firebox. "Bring me a flashlight!"

The sound from the fireplace became louder because the door was open, and a small shower of soot floated down from above. My son shone the light up the long tube of the chimney but saw nothing past the flue. Again the sound rattled down the chimney and throughout the house. By this time, the whole family was up, thinking we had a drummer on the roof performing a drum tattoo. We scrambled for our shoes and went outside to investigate.

As we came around the corner of the house, we saw the culprit sitting high and mighty on the wooden chimney surround where he could reach the metal chimney pot he was using as his personal drum. He was about ten inches from beak to tail tip, dressed in black-and-white plumage with a  bright red spot adorning his head like a crown. I ran back inside for the bird book and soon identified him as the Hairy Woodpecker, which is common in this area. *Birds of Alberta* had this to say:

> "The Hairy Woodpecker is easily confused with its smaller cousin (the Downey), so a second or third look is often required to confirm its identity. Looking like a Downey on steroids (*Oh yeah!!* I thought), the Hairy Woodpecker is slightly less common and more aloof. (Nothing aloof about this fellow, we all agreed as he set off another drum roll.) The Hairy Woodpecker does not sing during courtship,(the book continued,) instead it drums rhythmically on trees. Its courtship flights are equally unusual—this bird produces loud sounds by beating its wings against its flanks."

Just as I finished reading, there was an answering *rat-a-tat-tat* from somewhere on the neighbors property.

"Oh, great!" was my sons disgruntled comment. "There go the peaceful Sunday mornings! I would like to know how he discovered that our chimney pot makes a louder sound than the trees out back."

Since then, the drum tattoo on our chimney pot and that of our neighbor has become a regular occurrence, and we have learned to live with it for the three or four weeks of the mating season. My daughter, who lives in the city, also has a Hairy Woodpecker that has found that drumming on the metal lamppost in front of their house is also beneficial in calling for a mate. So their neighborhood also resounds with a drum tattoo in the stillness of a Sunday morning when all the world wants is an extra hour of sleep. These birds have adapted to manmade surroundings.

Adaptation. Now there is another interesting word! How do birds and animals learn to adapt to the encroaching, so-called civilization? The jackrabbit population has exploded in the city, where they take full advantage of the succulent plants we provide and the lack of natural predators. The rabbits' days of peaceful procreation may be numbered, however, because coyotes are now making inroads into well-populated areas, picking off those pesky rabbits or our pets, such as small dogs and cats, for their dinner. Cougars and even bears are losing their fear of man and are becoming common threats to children playing outdoors.

Perhaps the tattoo on the chimney is more than an irritation on a Sunday morning. Perhaps it is a wake-up call to look at what we are doing to nature by encroaching on the habitats of birds and animals when we build our houses. It is a call to think about what happens to those birds and animals when we use so-called modern farming methods and destroy natural areas of vegetation by tilling wall to wall on our acreage or when we apply pesticide.

God calls us to be masters of land, animals, and birds, but doesn't He also call us to be good stewards of those natural resources? My observation is that if we upset the natural order of things, there will be consequences, even if it is only the inconvenience of a noisy woodpecker on our chimney early one Sunday morning. When we encroach on nature too much, we can expect the animals and birds to adapt and use the manmade objects to suit their needs in order to survive.

I invite you to think about this Scripture from Deuteronomy 8:6-13:

> Observe the commands of the Lord your God, walking in his ways and revere him. For the Lord your God is bringing you into a good land—a land with streams and pools of water, with springs flowing in the valleys and the hills; a land with wheat and barley, vines and fig trees, pomegranates, olive oil and honey; a land where bread will not be scarce and you will lack for nothing; a land where the rocks are iron and you dig copper out of the hills. When you have eaten and are satisfied, praise the Lord, for the good land he has given you. Be careful that you do not forget the Lord your God, failing to observe his commands, his laws, and his decrees.

While I am not a radical nature nut, it makes sense to me that if we rob the land of its resources without regard for the consequences, we will lose something precious that God provided for our sustenance and enjoyment.

Sprinkles

"Grandma, can I have a doughnut with sprinkles? Please? Oh, *please*?" my little grandson asks every time we see a Tim Horton's doughnut shop.

I don't know about your children or grandchildren, but mine love sprinkles on anything. Somehow they transform mundane food into the extraordinary. So we have a collection of various hues and shapes of sprinkles in the cupboard next to the baking powder and the vanilla. It always amazes me to see the eyes of children grow round with excitement when I present a ho-hum muffin dressed up with a small amount of glaze and a few chocolate sprinkles on top or when I add some yellow chicks or pink piggy's to the top of the fruit salad. I stand back and just watch the food disappear simply because it had sprinkles on top.

Some sprinkles are very special. Recently, someone found a jar of silver sprinkles while shopping and have transformed the Valentine cookies this year into an amazing treat for the kindergarten class. The silver sprinkles also added an element of authenticity to a birthday cake that was transformed into a pirate's treasure chest spilling its treasure of candy necklaces, gold-wrapped chocolate coins, and jewel-like gumdrops onto a sandy shore made up of silver sand with chocolate rocks.

The uses for the sweet-colored treats are only limited by the imagination and have found they have the power to transform any day into a celebration. I have added them to a common pudding in honour of a good mark on a spelling test. The plain vanilla ice cream becomes a red explosion with a few raspberries and red sprinkles added to it. The joy these tiny, sweet treasures bring adds a touch of whimsy to a humdrum day and is well worth their cost. I have decorated plain vanilla cupcakes with orange icing and black bats and spiders for the school Halloween party, and the squeals of delight made the effort worthwhile. I recommend that every mother and grandmother keep a few sprinkles in the pantry and watch how they transform quarrelsome resistance into delighted cooperation at the dinner table.

When I was cleaning the dining room a week after the pirate birthday, I found a few silver sprinkles on the floor that had escaped the chubby pirates' mouths. I found myself thinking that God adds sprinkles to our lives, and all we have to do is open our hearts and minds to recognize them. I would like to share a few sprinkles that God has added to my life.

I opened the door to my country home and heard the trill of the house wren's song that instantly lifted my heart. I am privileged to see my grandchildren every day and hear their laughter as they play. I love the warm welcome I always receive from my little dog when I arrive home and the unexpected hugs I receive from a family member or a friend. Recently, I received a phone call from an old friend who I haven't seen in a long time, during which we caught up and shared a lot of laughter. And while in conversation with a new friend at a club meeting, we discovered many common interests and made plans to attend a music event.

A verse or two of poetry written by someone I have never met or a piece of artwork or photography from someone who has travelled far has lifted my spirits and changed my attitude as surely as if that person had come to my home and added sprinkles to my common bran muffin. God is not limited by time and space and He will use what was said or done by someone far away or long ago to inspire me. I have often read something by some obscure individual or seen a painting by some master that was just the right sprinkle to get me through a mediocre day. Just today, I saw that God had sprinkled wildflowers in the ditch and over the hill next to the road where I drive everyday. Then as I returned home, He had sprinkled a few clouds across the sunset, making it more amazing than usual with colours of purple, gold, and pink reflected by the towering ques.

On the day that six little children came to celebrate a pirate birthday with my grandson, I couldn't help thinking of Psalm 34: 8, 9, 11-14 as the children expressed their delight at the sweet treasures from the cake:

> O taste and see that the Lord is good;
> Blessed is the man who takes refuge in Him,
> Fear the Lord, you His saints,
> for those who fear Him lack nothing.
> Come, my children, listen to me;
> I will teach you the fear of the Lord.
> Whoever of you who loves life
> And desires to see many good days,
> Keep your tongue from evil
> And your lips from speaking lies.
> Turn from evil and do good;
> Seek peace and pursue it.

All we have to do is open our hearts and minds to find that our lives can be transformed from so-so into the "phantasmagorical," as my grandchildren would say, when we find God has added sprinkles to our lives.

I pray you will find God's special sprinkles in your life today!

The Wonder of It All

The other morning, I watched from the kitchen window as my six-year-old grandson squatted at the edge of the driveway, poking at something with a stick. Finally, my curiosity got the better of me, and I went out to investigate.

"I found an anthill, Grandma!" he said with the enthusiasm that can only be generated by a boy when he has discovered bugs. "Look at 'em go!" He poked at them once more.

Now it was up to me to ride to the rescue of the poor little creatures as their home of twigs and sand was being destroyed. "I see them, but they are not toys for you to play with. They are living creatures and have a home and family just like you do. How do you think you would feel if some huge beast came and stuck a stick in our windows?"

"But, Grandma, I just want to see how they live inside their house and what they do," he protested without malice.

After a little more observation and a further discussion, I convinced him that there were better ways to find out about ants than to destroy this ant nest and possibly kill the little creatures. We went inside to the computer and found a great source on the Internet for him to watch, and I also found a book about ants with great pictures. Last of all, I agreed that we would set up an ant farm after we went to the hobby shop the next time we went to town. The little plastic box with its clear windows would open a view into the ants' world and would give my grandson the pleasure of watching them without destroying their home. And then when he grew tired of them, they could be released to do what ants do.

Now I know that some think of ants as pests that invade our space, get into our food at picnics, and, worst-case scenario may even invade and destroy our wooden houses, but that was not part of today's lesson. I remembered a passage from the Bible that teaches us that God appreciated the industry of ants: "Go to the ant, o sluggard, consider her ways. Without having any chief, officer, or ruler, she prepares her bread in summer and gathers her food in harvest" (Proverbs 6:6-8).

As we watched the ants, I explained to my grandson that we should respect these little creatures because they don't need anyone to tell them to work hard to gather their food and build their home. We could learn a lesson or two from them and do as the old adage says, "Make hay while the sun shines," and learn to store against the day when the storms of life will rage. Ants are smart and know that when winter storms come, there will be no food to gather, and they will need shelter from the cold. They are smart in other ways too, because if one finds a source of food, such as an open jam jar left at a picnic, he will lead the rest of his family back to help gather the food. They also cooperate with one another in building intricate houses with rooms for different purposes, such as storage for food, a nursery for the babies, and places to rest. They also are neat and clean and have special worker ants that carry out the garbage and repair the tunnels.

As I observed the wonder on my grandson's face while he watched and learned about the ants, I remembered a verse from Christ's teachings about the wonder of children. I found many verses, but the ones from Mark 10:13-16 expressed what I was thinking of best. Christ said, "Let the little children come to me, and do not hinder them, for the kingdom of God belongs to such as these. I tell you the truth; anyone who will not receive the kingdom of God like a child will never enter it."

Let's examine the attributes of a child that Christ is looking for in us if we hope to enter the kingdom of God. Little children accept things they learn with a simple faith. They believe what you tell them until it is proven wrong. They are without guile, lust for power or worldly ambition and therefore have no ulterior motive for investigating things other than to learn. My observation is that they see things with the purity of the empty canvas upon which the artist has yet to leave his mark. The younger ones are without pride and are not affected by the trends and fashions of this world. These things are learned from those around them, so God cautions us in Matthew 18:3-7:

> Therefore, whoever humbles himself like this child is the greatest in the kingdom of heaven. And whoever welcomes a little child like this in my name welcomes me. But if anyone causes one of these little ones who believe in me to sin, it would be better for him to have a millstone hung around his neck and to be drowned in the depths of the sea. Woe to the world because of the things that cause people to sin! Such things must come, but woe to the man through whom they come!

Over the next couple of days, I thought about how wonderful it was to experience the world through a child's eyes once more and what a great responsibility it is to raise a child. We "sophisticated" adults become so caught up in the rush of business and puffed up by our own accomplishments that we don't take time to appreciate the simple wonders of nature. We become jaded by the vast amounts of knowledge we accumulate and become desensitized by the sights and sounds we are bombarded with all day long every day through media and the Internet. I challenge you today to turn off the radio, the television, and the computer. Take a child by the hand, and go for a nature walk. I promise that you will learn once more to see the wonders of God's kingdom.

I leave you with this passage from Psalm 127:3-5:

> Sons are a heritage from the Lord, children a reward from him. Like arrows in the hand of the warrior are the sons born in one's youth. Blessed is the man whose quiver is full of them. They will not be put to shame when they contend with their enemies in the gate.

Hidden in Plain View

Have you ever sent someone, perhaps a child or a spouse, to retrieve a specific article for you, only for him or her to claim he or she cannot see the article at all? Even though you give further instructions and an exact description, they still claim they cannot find it. Finally, after some minutes and more yelling, which may include questions, such as "Are you sure it is in here?" and statements that question your sanity, you give up in a fit of frustration and go to the cupboard yourself. After you use precious minutes to climb up or down some stairs, you find the article right where you said it was!

Why is it that people develop schetoma, or psychological blindness, when they are looking directly at a common object? I once saw a secretary trip over her own garbage can that had been sitting in the same location beside her desk for two years. She claimed she did not see it as she hurried to respond to her boss's urgent call. In my case, the article I needed did everything, except jump up and down and wave. It was exactly as I had described it, colour and shape, and was located exactly where I had told my husband it was, but he was still unable to see it. So I ask, why is this so?

Some psychologists suggest that people often have a preconceived idea of what an article should look like, and so if it does not match their mental picture, they cannot see the article. Another psychologist said that if we are distracted, we often don't see common articles that we see every day. We can drive down the same street everyday, past the same shops and houses, but if someone asked us to give the exact location of one of those shops, we couldn't tell them. We own a small dry cleaning plant, and the other day, I had a lady tell me she must have been in our strip mall a hundred times but did not know we were there until she had spilled her wine during dinner and a friend told her to come to us. I could confirm this because I recognized her from the many times I had seen her walk by.

If we develop blindness to the object we walk by everyday, is it any wonder that so many of us cannot see God? If we open our spiritual eyes, we will find Him everywhere, hidden in plain view. He may not appear exactly like our preconceived ideas, and we may have to take a fresh approach to our everyday spiritual understanding of what God looks like. I have said that there has never been a time in my life when I did not know God, so let me tell you some of the places I have found Him hidden in plain view.

Last night as I drove home through the dark clouds and lightening of an impending storm, I saw the mighty power of the Creator. I was feeling so tired and a bit depressed after a long day's work, but when I came over the hill into the little valley where we live, I found it bathed in the golden glow of a glorious sunset with tones of peach, gold, and soft purple transforming the sky and clouds. When I called the children to see the beautiful sunset that had revived my spirit, my granddaughter said it was like the colours of a ripe peach, only better, because it was God sending us light from heaven.

This morning, I found Him sailing on the fresh morning breeze with the wispy, white clouds and the tangy fragrance of the pine forest.

I see his playful nature in the squirrels that come looking for nuts in the feeder outside my kitchen window and I hear His voice in the call of the Canada geese flying over head.

His good humour was revealed as I listened to the laughter of the children at play in the schoolyard.

I find Him in the unconditional love of my little dog and in her patience and forgiveness when I am late coming home to feed her.

Last week, I saw His generosity among the group of volunteers stuffing backpacks with school supplies for children of poor families who cannot afford all those supplies.

For several years now, we have been involved with a program called Inn from the Cold, which houses homeless people in church basements. Many of those who come have jobs but are not making enough money for a security deposit on an apartment. There I see the hands and feet of Jesus at work and feel His love among the volunteers who set up cots and prepare tables of food for these people. We all know it's a hostile world for the poor, so I'm reminded of a verse from Psalm 23: 5, "You prepare a table before me in the presence of my enemies."

I felt Christ's concern for the children when a teacher I know made arrangements to meet with a struggling student after school so she could tutor him in math. She will not be paid for the time she spends, but her reward will be seeing the child's life changed forever because of his improved math skills. Who knows what that child might become because someone took the time to help and encourage him?

I saw Him in the native dancers and drummers who participated in the powwow given in remembrance of the elements of the Great Creator: earth, air, fire, and water. I saw His face reflected in the kind, chiseled features of the elder who gave thanks before the celebration.

I saw His beauty reflected in Beauvais Lake, where we spent a lovely day fishing, and I saw His nature defined in an old man's kindness as he told us where to catch more fish. The experience was a little like Christ telling his disciples to cast the net on the other side of the boat.

I felt His power in the strength and the force of the windstorm that blew the fall leaves from the trees.

When we came back to the city, I saw His healing power on the street among the health workers of the mobile hospital bus that comes to serve the homeless and 'girls of the evening'. They were offering shelter from the cold, warm mittens and hats, free food, and medical attention as well as a way out of that life style.

I see evidence of His providence and His love in the piles of work He has provided our business so that we might earn enough for our daily bread.

I see His love reflected in the love two newlyweds share as they bring the wedding gown to our dry cleaning plant.

I saw His righteous anger when I watched a policeman make an arrest.

I find God everywhere in everything I experience, both good and bad, for He also allows us to suffer so we might learn to depend more fully upon His strength.

Today, I saw His joy in the shining faces of the church members as they sang His praises on this fine Sunday morning.

And last of all, I taste His body and blood given in sacrifice for my sins in the bread and wine we share at communion.

Where do you see Him today?

"Ask and it will be given to you; seek and you will find; knock and it will be opened to you. For everyone who asks receives; he who seeks finds; and to him who knocks, the door will be opened" (Matthew 7:7).

The Circle of Life

The little boy sat in the stern of the small aluminum boat bundled in a life jacket with his pack and fishing rod at his side, waiting for his dad to finish loading his gear. At last, Dad stepped into the boat and pushed off from the dock. When they were far enough away, Dad turned the boat around with the paddle and then started the motor. The little boy watched the dock, his mother, and sister get smaller and smaller as the boat putted across the lake.

When they reached a spot where some rocks were piled near the shore, Dad stopped the motor and steadied the boat with an oar. He poured a cup of coffee for himself and a cup of hot chocolate for his son and then began to ready the fishing lines.

"What kind of bait shall we try? What do you think will tickle their fancy this morning?"

"Tickle, Daddy? Do I have to tickle the fish? That will be pretty hard when they're in the water and I'm up here in the boat. I might fall in." This was his first fishing trip, and he didn't understand what his dad was talking about.

"Well, son, what I meant was that we will have to figure out what kind of food the fish are looking for this morning. Then we'll put that on our hooks so we can catch them."

So began the ritual of a man and a boy with a fishing rod; a ritual as old as time and as important as any rite of passage in a school of higher learning. This is the school of life where lessons, perhaps more important than those taught in school, are passed from one generation to the next.

In this case, the dad is my son, Timothy Axel, who learned the lessons of fishing and life from his grandfather, Axel

Joseph, in this same boat with its red stripe on this same lake at Beaver Mines. The old aluminum boat travelled in those days on top of the Fury, a red-and-white car with enough horsepower to pull the boat and the little trailer stuffed with all the gear for a weeklong camping trip more than thirty years ago. These days, the boat, now a little battered and scratched, travels on top of the Dodge van with all the gear that a family of four needs for a week of camping and fishing jammed inside.

Off they go, Dad and son, Sven Axel, to catch a fish or perhaps not. What is guaranteed, however, is that they will catch the time to build relationship and talk about some of the important things of life that a boy can only learn from his dad while they are gently bobbing up and down on a beautiful, calm lake. The early morning sun is sparkling on the waves, and the fresh, pine-scented breeze is tickling their senses. They will share moments when nothing is more important than watching the bald eagle soaring overhead in a sky so blue it hurts the eyes. They will see a demonstration of patience by watching the great blue heron, which is a much better fisher than the man or his son will ever be. They will share simple pleasure as they watch the great bird wade out to catch a fish down at the shallows.

Later, they will talk of things they would like to do in the future while impatiently scorching hot dogs over a fire that is still burning too hot, and then they'll snuggle with Mom and sister, Signe, under a blanket as they count the stars that wink at them through the tree branches. They'll joke about how the Big One got away while drinking hot chocolate and devouring s'mores made over the glowing, hot coals of the campfire.

I think of Grandfather these days because it has been five years since he passed on to the great fishing hole beyond.

I remember his kind ways and stern teachings with more fondness and much more appreciation now that I am a grandmother. The following poem, written by Edgar A. Guest, always reminds me of him because he taught my son, now Dad, Timothy Axel to fish when he was Sven's age:

A Boy and His Dad

A boy and his dad on a fishing trip
There is a glorious fellowship!
Father and son and the open sky
And the white clouds lazily drifting by,
And the laughing stream as it runs along
With the clicking reel like a martial song.
And the father teaching the youngster gay
How to land a fish in the sportsman's way.

I fancy I hear them talking there
In an open boat, and the speech is fair;
And the boy is learning the ways of men
From the finest man in his youthful ken.
Kings to the youngster, cannot compare
With the gentle father who's with him there.
And the greatest mind the human race
Not for one minute could take his place.

Which is happier, man or boy?
The soul of the father is steeped in joy,
For he's finding out to his heart's delight
That his son is fit for the future fight.
He is learning the glorious depths of him.
And the thoughts he thinks and his every whim,
And he shall discover, when night comes on.
How close he has grown to his little son.

I write this today, March 20, 2011, in memory of a good man, Grandpa Axel; teacher, father, and grandfather, who passed away on this day five years ago.

Never Give Up!

About four years ago, a wee fawn was born behind the house in a nest of tall grass under the aspen trees on the acreage we call Aspen Croft. Throughout that summer, the doe would follow the same path through the yard on her way to the water in the ravine with the fawn by her side. She would often lead the fawn to a hiding place near where she had been born and leave her there to sleep while she went off to graze.

I often came face-to-face with the doe and her young when I was out in the yard. I would stop what I was doing, make eye contact with them, and allow them to pass without frightening them. The fawn grew rapidly, and it was such a pleasure watching little "Faline," as we had come to call her, play with the other fawns as they began to do things independently from their mothers.

That year, I planted pansies in the pots on my deck. When I had finished, I washed the deck and took my tools back to the garage. When I returned to view my handiwork, I found both doe and fawn on the deck, nibbling the pansy blossoms like a tray of hors d'oeuvres. They looked so hilarious and guilty with evidence of their misdemeanor dangling from their mouths that I could not be angry. After a moment's hesitation, during which we locked eyes and wills, there was a mad scramble as they jumped off the steps, overturning some pots in the process.

That was the beginning of my relationship with this lovely creature, Faline. Over the next year, she came often to nibble the blossoms from my flowerbeds and poke her nose through the page wire around the garden to pull the irresistible tiny, new peapods from the plants.

The next spring, I put a gate on the deck and planted the peas further toward the centre of the garden. I also planted flowers that were not quite so tasty in the flowerbeds. She still came to visit and would stare at the house, waiting for me to make eye contact when I came out. Then she would raise her white, fluffy tail and bound away a short distance before she continued grazing. I love the deer that abound in the neighborhood, and I think she could sense that I was not a threat to her. She was picture-perfect with her large, liquid eyes and sleek, new coat that glistened red against the verdant green of the meadow on the south side of the house.

That winter was very cold for long periods. The snow came early and lay in a deep, even blanket by Christmas. We chopped up the Halloween pumpkin and some apples and carrots and put them out to supplement the grass the herd found by digging through the snow.

Despite the hard winter that spring, she came down the old trail looking sleek and fat. One morning soon after that, we saw her near where she had been born with not one but two beautiful, dappled fawns close by her side. All spring and summer, she travelled through the neighborhood, sticking close to the yards where she and her young would be protected from the coyote pack that lived in the pasture behind our lot. We would watch eagerly for a glimpse of her dappled twins. By August, they had grown into gangly teenagers with minds of their own. We would see them romping through the trees playing reindeer games with the other fawns, and they seemed to wander farther and farther away from their mother.

In September, Faline and her twins went to the pasture where the new crop of oats was an irresistible addition to their diet. We had seen the coyote pack there in the evenings and knew they had increased in number by the volume of their song. They had a new batch of pups that had to be fed and taught to hunt for themselves. I was afraid for the young fawns, but I also accepted that nature provides without favour.

One Saturday morning about a week later, Faline came hobbling into the yard, badly injured, which brought back memories of my pet ewe and her lamb that had been attacked by coyotes when I was ten. Faline's front left leg was dangling at a strange angle, and she had a huge gash on her shoulder. I could see that she had injuries to her back as well where huge clumps of fur were missing or standing up at odd angles around the wounds. What was even more distressing was that now only one fawn followed her and nursed when she stood still.

I phoned Fish and Game, but they would do nothing. The lady who answered said they did not have a budget that included nursing every deer that was found injured. She told me that we could put her down if she became worse, but she advised me to wait and see. So we waited and were amazed to see that Faline not only healed but also continued to nurse and clean her one remaining fawn.

Faline grew round and sleek as summer neared its close and weaned the fawn. Through the fall and winter, we saw her with the other does, and although she was slower, she managed to tag along with the herd, even learning to leap and run again. In the spring, we were amazed to see her in the yard again, healthy once more despite her shoulder being twisted and dislocated. She grazed in and around my flowerbeds all spring; I did not have the heart to shoo her away.

One Sunday morning in early June, Faline came into the yard. I was washing dishes, so I had ample time to watch her as she passed in front of the house. She did not seem her usual self. She showed no interest in the green spring grass and did not stop to nibble the succulent buds on the rosebush as had been her habit. She hobbled a few steps and then stopped to look around, went a few more steps, and repeated the process. Finally, she made her way to the centre of the small grove of trees about thirty feet from the deck and lay down among the rosebushes and grass that comprise the undergrowth.

I called the rest of the family to bring the binoculars, as I figured she was about to deliver a fawn in our yard. We watched closely as the sun made its way across the summer sky. About three o'clock, we saw her stand and shake herself. After another two hours, we were finally rewarded with our first glimpse of the miracle. She brought her tiny, new, dappled baby toward the house as if to show it off and say, "See? I survived. And just look at this new baby!"

Faline took about another two hours to clean the baby very carefully, nurse it, and then push it along with her nose until she reached the spot where she herself had been born. There she bedded it down for the night and went off to graze and get water. My grandchildren were amazed at the whole process, and we took many pictures that day and more as the little one grew throughout the summer.

The miracle of her healing and the birth of her new fawn does not end there, however. June was very late in the season for a fawn to be born, and the other fawns were head-and-shoulders ahead for the remainder of the summer. As a result, Faline was still nursing her babe when fall came and hunting season and the rut began. One evening, we heard shots ring through the valley where we live that seemed to come from the ranch that borders our land over the hill to the west. I hoped it was not directed at Faline and her still dependent fawn and went to bed disquieted.

I did not see Faline for many days. In fact, all the deer had disappeared, as they often do during hunting season, keeping clear of humans and travelling in ravines where dense brush provides cover for them.

Then about the middle of November, on a day that was unseasonably warm, Faline came ambling into the yard with her ungainly gait that distinguished her from the other does and in her wake came her own small fawn and another slightly larger one. When she reached the safety of the yard, she stopped to nurse both fawns in plain view of the house. This amazingly courageous and tenacious animal had adopted another motherless baby and continues to watch over them even now as, once more, December snow lies two feet deep in our yard and the temperatures dip to minus thirty. They come to paw their way down to the succulent lawn grass and search out the apple treats we throw into the flowerbeds. They have grown round and fat while feeding on the abundant crops in the neighborhood, and a long, warm fall gave them adequate time to grow and produce thick, warm coats against the winter chill. I must say, I hold great hope of seeing another baby born next spring, for I saw that our Faline had attracted a healthy-looking buck that same week in November when she reappeared with two fawns in tow.

Watching this doe has been a huge inspiration for me as we near the end of this year. We have faced uncertain financial times in the world along with the other problems of ill health, accidents, and just plain foolishness that we humans get ourselves into. When I see Faline and think of what she has endured and the loyalty and love she has displayed as a mother to her own offspring and others', I can say that I am inspired to love more deeply, live more fully, and never give up! I am reminded of the doe when I read Psalm 18:30-33:

> As for God, his way is perfect; the word of the Lord is flawless. He is a shield for all who take refuge in him. For who is God beside the Lord? And who is the Rock except our God? It is God who arms me with strength and makes my way perfect. He makes my feet like the feet of a deer; he enables me to stand firm on the heights.

And the more common reference to deer from Psalm 42:1, "As the deer pants for streams of water, so my soul pants for you, O God."

The psalmist wrote Psalms 42-72 when he was in great distress, perhaps suffering from depression. So I believe he could relate to the deer who graze near water because the grass is more succulent, and like an injured deer which often beds down near water because it knows it will need water in order to heal, he wanted to be near God where he would regain strength. So we too need to come to the living water of the Word of God in times of distress.

Blessing in Disguise

I have been suffering from bronchitis for about four weeks now. I have hacked and coughed, sneezed and blown my nose until I felt and looked a wreck. I have swallowed enough of that awful tasting Buckley's cough syrup to sail a ship on and sucked enough cough drops to unclog an elephant's nose, and I want to retch at the thought of taking one more thing that tastes medicinal. I almost called this story "AHHHCHOO!" until yesterday morning, when I woke up to find the worst of the symptoms *gone* except for that lingering, dry hacking cough. You know the kind I mean, that dry tickle that sends you into paroxysms of coughing just as you answer the telephone or pick up a dish of food or relax into REM sleep.

Last night, I took all the medication once more, hoping to quell that tickle, and felt pretty confident that I could get a good night's sleep. I read until I was sleepy, closed the book, removed my glasses, and turned out the light at about ten.

But to my dismay at about two a.m., I was jerked out of a deep sleep by another coughing fit. My chest went into spasm, and after about three hacking coughs, I knew I needed a drink of water and another dose of cough syrup. On went the light so I wouldn't trip over my little dog, Missy, who has taken to sleeping on a cushion beside my bed.

By the time I had the coughing under control; Missy was awake and was doing a dance while whining by the bedroom door, asking to go out.

I groaned. "Are you sure, dog? Do you really need to go out in the dark at *two-thirty* in the morning? It's cold out there, and the coyotes are out and about at this time!" But being of a certain age myself, I understood Missy's urgency and quickly slipped on a warm housecoat for the trip down the stairs and outside.

Missy made her hesitant way in the dark, down the front steps to the walk leading around the garage. That was when I noticed her head come up, sniffing as she faced into the late night breeze, and a deep rumble emanated from her throat. Now, I know she doesn't see very well any more, but there is definitely nothing wrong with her sense of smell, so I became concerned as she continued that low-pitched warning growl.

I went down the steps to investigate. When I got to the edge of the garage and was facing into the breeze myself, I realized what she was growling about. There was the definite "odeur de skunk" floating on the breeze, and to my surprise, I saw the garage door was wide open. My grandchildren had been out riding their bikes earlier in the evening, and one of the wheels was sticking out too far, preventing the door from closing. I panicked, thinking that perhaps the skunk had found its way into the garage.

Alarmed, I scrambled back into the house to the interior door to the garage. Because we live in bear country, we have been warned by Fish and Game officers to keep all garbage in the garage until pick-up day so we do not attract critters needlessly. I learned from growing up on the farm that skunks love garbage and try to find a warm den in the fall.

My next thought was that perhaps our odoriferous little friend had already invaded the garage, attracted by the smell of the oh-so-tasty kitchen scraps. I grabbed the broom and opened the interior door slowly. In retrospect, I really don't know what good the broom would have been, but weapon in hand, I hesitantly turned on the light, expecting to catch a black-and-white "wood pussy" tearing up the garbage bags. I sighed with relief when I saw that the coast was clear and the bags were still intact. Just to make sure our little friend wasn't hiding someplace, I clapped my hands and beat on the side of a bucket with the broom, hoping that the noise would alert the little fellow and give him plenty of time to exit stage left before I moved the bike and made another attempt at closing the door.

By that time, Missy was back from her night adventure, scratching to come in. When we finally got back upstairs and into bed, the clock said 3:10. My heart was doing double time, and I was wide-awake from the cold and excitement. I flipped and flopped for a few minutes in the dark, trying to get warm and calm, but finally gave up, turned the light back on, hoping to read myself to sleep once again.

Now, I don't know if I just had an overactive imagination triggered by the night's events or if there really was an animal outside, but in the stillness of the night, I was sure I heard animal sounds from the backyard near the fire pit. By this time, it was nearing four a.m., and I could definitely smell skunk on the night air coming through my open window. I arose once more and turned off the light so I might be able to see the little marauder by moonlight, if he was indeed out there in the woodpile. The moon, however, had set by this time, so being unable to see anything but general shapes of logs and bushes, I finally gave up the watch and returned to my bed. The LED display on my bedside clock now indicated it was 4:30, and I lay awake for another half hour before I finally dozed off into a fitful sleep until the alarm went off at seven.

I awoke listless, groggy, and with a head that felt big as a pumpkin, so I was more than a bit out of sorts when I got the grandchildren up for breakfast. They were out of sorts as well, resisting everything I asked them to do, but we finally got through breakfast, face-washing, and teeth-brushing with only a couple of minutes to spare before it was time to leave for school. I was still grouchy as I drove the children to school.

While I was dropping them off, I ran into a neighbor from the next lot who told me that she, too, was out of sorts because they had had an unwanted visitor during the night. They had been awakened by their dog's frantic barking, and in the morning, they had found their garden and berry patch in shambles, bird feeders tipped, and long scratch marks on the large poplar tree at the end of their drive—all evidence that a large black bear had been looking for food during the night. I promised to keep eyes and ears open when we were out and about because you don't want to surprise a grouchy, hungry bear that is looking for berries and such in order to fatten up before hibernation.

As I drove away, I wondered what might have happened if I had remained soundly asleep instead of being awakened by my irritating coughing spell. What would have happened if our friendly neighborhood skunk and Bruno the bear had both been attracted to our open garage by the promise of dinner "a la garbage"? Then I began to laugh as I imagined the proverbial Mexican standoff that might have taken place in the wee hours of the morning if I had not closed the garage door. We would probably have had the most messed up, foul-smelling garage in the entire neighborhood courtesy of one very bad-tempered bear and one very socially offensive skunk. Still laughing, I realized that it was fortunate that my coughing had awakened me and that Missy took me on a midnight ramble. Slowly, my attitude about the events of the night began to change. I became thankful that potential disaster had been averted.

We often rail at the events that disturb our well-ordered lives, our beauty sleep, or our plans, but we don't often think about what other events may have happened if the interruption had not occurred. Was my sleep interrupted serendipitously, or was it divine intervention that caused me to wake up coughing? Worst-case scenario, we would have had a ruckus in the garage that would have awakened us anyway, and then there would have been a very large, smelly mess to clean up.

So that coughing fit and midnight ramble were really blessings in disguise.

Because of this incident, I began to think of other more serious incidents that seemed to indicate that God takes an interest in our comings and goings. Here are a few of the incredible stories where the "intervention" saved someone from disaster.

We had a great-grandfather who missed sailing on the Titanic because his best friend and travelling companion had fallen ill. Not wanting to sail without his friend, he sold their tickets and waited for him to recover. At the time, he was not too happy about missing that great adventure. But in retrospect, here we are, three generations of a family that would most likely not exist if not for what he called "divine intervention" that saved his life.

I have a friend who narrowly missed being hit by a drunk driver who ran a red light because she stopped to take a phone call. She watched in horror from her spot at the side of the road as the car which had been behind her was broadsided when it took what would have been her place in the traffic going through the intersection. She has never taken an interruption or, as she calls it, "intervention" for granted ever since.

On the tenth anniversary of 9/11, we all heard stories from survivors of that disaster. There were some individuals who missed a train or stayed home that day because they had a cold. Perhaps the most touching story was that of a father who is alive today because he took the morning off to go with his wife to their son's first day of kindergarten.

Instead of rushing that morning, one gentleman decided to buy coffee and muffins for his staff, but the line was extra long so he missed his train. What are the odds that these things happened by chance? Or did these interventions happen because the Divine has a plan for their lives?

There is no one particular verse in the Bible that indicates that God intervenes in this way. However, we are assured of His divine providence in our lives in many stories, beginning with the story of Abraham who trusted God to provide a lamb even though God had commanded him to go to Moriah to sacrifice his son, Isaac. God did intervene. Because of Abraham's unquestioning obedience, God provided a ram that Abraham found caught by its horns in a thicket.

In Psalm 8:3-4, David gives voice to his belief that God intervenes in our lives as he says, "When I consider your heavens, the work of your fingers, the moon and the stars, which you have set in place, what is man that you are mindful of him, the son of man that you care for him?" And in Matthew 5:44-45, we are told, "God cares for all mankind and causes the sun to rise on the evil and the good and sends rain to fall on the fields of all; the wicked as well as the righteous."

We are also reminded through the story of Joseph in Genesis 37-50 of how God used the incidents of his life, even the malicious jealousy of his brothers, to move him from the fields of his homeland to a place of power in faraway in Egypt. Because of that he became powerful under Pharaoh, thus allowing Joseph to provide food and safety for his family during the famine. In this story, Joseph became the salvation of his family in spite all the evil his brothers had done to him. We see how God intervened, using the evil intent of man and changing it into a fortuitous ending for the family. This story has been touted as the forerunner to the life of Christ. We soon realize that the purpose of God's intervention and providence is the ultimate redemption of humanity.

When I looked for a definition of the words *divine intervention*, I found this statement in the Bible Dictionary: "The foreseeing and guardianship of God over His creatures—a manifestation of His divine care or direction." This statement describes what I believe. Some would say that such things are simply coincidence or having good luck, but I know without a doubt that some of the events that have changed my life's path, although irritating at the time, were His divine intervention and so were blessings in disguise!

Unconditional Love

Last weekend the "Boys" went hunting for big game. "Boys" is what we call my son and his friends, but they are really mature men in their forties. Six of them have been friends for more than twenty years, and you can usually find two or three of them together on any given weekend. Their wives often joke about their close relationship saying they spend more time with each other than they do with their respective families. We all know, however, that they are loyal and true friends who will drop everything to help each other or the others' families without reserve. They each have special talents and skills that they share with each other, and we are all better off because of their friendship.

They did not find game on their hunting trip, but what they did find was a dog. As they drove down a secluded road, they saw a flash of white-and-brown fur in the ditch. At first, they thought it was a coyote and slowed down to see for sure. There she was, a beautiful collie, obviously well trained, and although injured and close to death, she responded to their call. She came limping out of the ditch, wagging her tail, skinny and dirty but trusting.

All indications were that she had been in the same spot for many days, waiting for her master's return. The boys were not willing to leave her there to suffer attack and death from the coyotes howling nearby, so they made a plan to rescue her. They looked for some form of identification on her, and finding none, they carefully loaded her into the back of the truck to take her to the nearest veterinarian. However, the country vet was not interested in helping them, so they brought her to a pet hospital in the city, where they discovered she had been hit by a car and suffered severe injuries to her pelvis. Even though she was severely injured and had not been fed for some time, she displayed a loving personality, wagging her tail in appreciation of the kindness, food, and water. She was a border collie and was obviously well trained, so the vet agreed to take her in, do the surgery, and put her up for adoption.

Border collies are known for their intelligence and loyalty. They are most commonly used for herding sheep and cattle, but in recent years, they have been used to keep geese off the runways of large airports. If you have a border collie, you have one of the best friends you could ever have.

When I was about five, we received a collie pup from a neighbor who was breeding and training them as cattle dogs. They are eager to please, and with their superior intelligence, they are easy to train, so it didn't take long for this pup to become a valuable asset on our farm.

Aside from his ability to herd cattle, he became my best friend. I took my afternoon nap with my head resting on his side and ran over the hills, exploring, with him as my companion. My mother said she never worried about where I was when the collie was with me.

By the time he was three, he was unusually well trained and would round up and bring home the four milk cows out of a herd of forty at my father's command. He would help round up the chickens in the evening and would find and stand guard over articles, such as tools or clothing, left in the garden or field.

Collie, as we called him, became somewhat of a legend. The local cattlemen asked my dad and him to accompany them for the fall cattle drive, and Dad was often asked to demonstrate Collie's talents to visiting friends and neighbors. Dogs came and went throughout our years on the farm, but Collie will always stand out as the most loving and intelligent of them all. When my son came home from the hunting trip and shared the story of this lost and abused dog, memories of my childhood companion came flooding back. My impulse was to adopt this stray and give it the love and care a dog of this breed deserves.

Coincidentally, I was doing a study on the unconditional love of God at this time, and my son and his friends' compassion for this dog reminded me of the story of the Good Samaritan, in which a man, himself an outcast because of his nationality, demonstrates that love by stopping to help a stranger who had been robbed and beaten. The Samaritan administered first aid, dressed his wounds, and then took him to an inn, where he paid for his care and lodging. As followers of Christ, we are all called to these acts of kindness and selfless love.

Someone once made the statement that there is no such thing as unconditional love among mankind. We could study relationships like the one between siblings or that of a mother and child, but even there the love comes fraught with rules, arguments, and expectations. Even the best marriage has problems that arise from unfulfilled dreams and broken promises. They don't say that dogs are man's best friend without good reason, and this dog, in spite of being injured and deserted by man, was still willing to forgive and offer friendship. I once heard this joke: "If you want to find out who your best friend is, try locking your wife and your dog in the garage for about two hours. Then see which one will be happy to see you when you come to let them out."

But on a serious note, if we are looking for an example of unconditional love, I believe it will be nearly impossible to find among human beings. My premise is that only in our relationship with our heavenly Father can we find unconditional love. The best example of that love is found in the Scriptures, which tell us that God sent us his Son, Jesus, to die, becoming the propitiation for our sins while we were still sinners. He didn't wait for us to come to Him, repenting first. No, He forgave us before we even asked!

The most common portion of the Bible that gives us a formula for this love is found in 1 Corinthians 13:1-8, which is often spoken in marriage services:

> If I speak in tongues of men and angels, but have not love, I am only a resounding gong or a clanging cymbal. If I have the gift of prophecy and can fathom all mysteries and all knowledge, and if I have faith that can move mountains but have not love, I am nothing. If I give all I posses to the poor and surrender my body to the flames, but have not love, I gain nothing. Love is patient, love is kind. It does not envy, it does not boast, it is not proud. It is not rude, it is not self-seeking, it is not easily angered, it keeps no record of wrongs. Love does not delight in evil but rejoices with truth. It always protects, always trusts, always hopes, always perseveres. Love never fails!

I wonder how many of us really stop to think about the criteria these verses impart. More than that, how many of us try to put what they teach into practice in our daily lives? As I studied these verses, I came to the conclusion, for what it's worth, that the closest example of unconditional love we can find on this earth is the forgiveness, love, and loyalty a dog offers to its master.

Here Comes the Rain

My journal entry for this morning, Tuesday, September 14, says, "Here comes the rain. The change in temperature and even the smell during the last week definitely reminds me that fall is coming. In fact, it reminds me of fall in England. The scent of wet, decaying leaves with just a hint of mint that comes drifting on the air currents from the kitchen garden has the power to transport me back to my friend's house in Winchester, England."

I have been thinking of my friends who live in England and the lovely week that I spent with them. They made my trip really special and interesting by dropping everything to be my tour guides and hosts. We visited many of the national historic places, such as The New Forest, where we had lunch at one of the oldest shipbuilding yards in a pub called Bucklers Hard. We spent a very rainy day at Oxford where we saw its famous university, ancient coffeehouses, and interesting Street Theatre. The next day, we travelled to a typical old English village in Devon called Lulworth, where we had high tea in the courtyard of an inn with a thatched roof and chickens in the garden. I will never forget the day we spent at Stonehenge and the lunch of meat pies from Cornwall. But the highlight for me was the day we toured London and Westminster Abbey.

The Abbey has always been to me the symbol of Britain because of its historical connection to the Monarchy, so I was really looking forward to that visit. On Tuesday, September 12, 1999, it was drizzling when we left for the train station in Winchester. Travelling to London by train early in the morning allowed us to make the most of the day.

It was a lovely, warm day by the time we arrived in London, so we caught one of those red double-decker buses for a tour of Old London, where we rode on the open upper deck. We saw Buckingham Palace, landmarks that formed the original walled city and the site of the old marketplace as well as the Tower Bridge and the Globe Theatre where Shakespeare's plays were held. We passed by Big Ben on time to hear the clock strike twelve that left my ears ringing for an hour. The tour ended near the Abbey around noon, so we found a beautiful, old pub where we had a typical lunch of fish and chips. Then we lined up for the guided tour of Westminster Abbey.

Inside, the history of the Abbey was delivered by another efficient and well informed local tour guide who gave us so many facts and figures. I knew I would never remember them all, so I just let it all go in one ear and out the other in order to absorb the sights, sounds and sensations. Awe at the immensity of structure and wonder at the skill of the craftsmen washed over me as we walked. However, I did hear that the Abbey has been a shrine since the year 616 AD when a fisherman saw a vision of Saint Peter near the site and I was awestruck when I walked by the Shrine of Saint Edward the Confessor and the tombs of Elizabeth I and her stepsister Mary, Queen of Scots. As we continued over the ancient stone floor, we came to the poet's corner where I saw many familiar names, including Geoffrey Chaucer, Charles Dickens, Rudyard Kipling, Alfred Lord Tennyson, and a plaque commemorating Shakespeare although he is not buried there and I began to cry, simply overwhelmed.

At the end of the tour, we stood beneath the window commemorating the Battle of Britain near the tomb of the Unknown Soldier. This soldier fought and died in World War I and was buried here on Armistice Day, November 11, 1920, to honour those lost in the Great War of 1914-1918. His body was brought from France along with one hundred barrels of soil from where he had fallen, which was buried with him beneath a black marble slab from Belgium. The gold lettering on the slab is made of shell casings collected from the fields of France. It has become tradition for any Royal bride who is married in the Abbey to leave her bouquet there on the tomb at the end of the ceremony. Recently the memories of that tour returned to me as I watched with some emotion as Prince William and his bride, Katherine, stopped there after their wedding ceremony for her to leave her bouquet on the tomb.

On that day during the tour, as I turned around slowly to take in the immensity of this gothic building and its splendor, I could not contain the wellspring of emotion I was feeling. The tears continued to flow, and my friend became dismayed. "Why are you crying?" she asked, putting a comforting arm around my shoulders. The only words I could choke out through the sobs were, "They're real!"

We went to sit in a quiet corner of the College Garden attached to the nave where I finally grew calm enough to explain. I told her I was overwhelmed at the presence of the kings, queens, poets, and statesmen who were buried there and seemed to continue to have a real presence there within those hallowed walls. It was almost as if I could hear the whisper of silk, the murmur of their prayers, and the rustle of their gowns sweeping along the ancient corridors of the transept even though most had been buried here centuries before. Furthermore, I had just realized that they were not just characters from the pages of a history book but were real individual souls who had lived, loved, shared food and fellowship, and offered up their prayers near this very spot. The kings and queens whose names and dates of reign I had had to memorize, with some reluctance, in school had been crowned here, attended services with their families here, and made important decisions here that still affect my life, even now, in the twenty-first century. And now they are buried here, where I could still see their tombs.

Some had lived their entire lives not more than twenty miles from this site. People, whose works of art and literature I had studied in school and still admire had struggled to put words on paper here, perhaps even on the very bench where I sat with my friend in the oldest garden in all Britannia. I explained that I was overwhelmed by the realization that they had really lived and that I was here where their bodies still rested within the confines of these sacred walls. Soon, my friend began to understand my tears and confided that she had also felt very emotional when she had first come here but had grown accustomed to the historical significance of the ancient buildings because there are so many located in every town in England.

I learned that the proper name for this edifice is The Collegiate Church of Saint Peter and is called a "Royal Peculiar" because it is under the jurisdiction of the Queen and Chapter and is subject only to the Sovereign. It was named a World Heritage site in 1987 and is a must-see if you are in London. But there is for me a feeling of the presence of God and those who served their country there, so bring Kleenex if you are inclined to be, as I was, overwhelmed by the history and grandeur of this ornate gothic structure. Because I had some experience with building while helping my father do renovations to our house on the farm, I stood awestruck by the skill of the craftsmen who had built this huge stone structure during a time when everything was handcrafted and I wondered at how they managed to move the huge blocks of stone into place. My cheeks were still wet with tears as I looked back at this immense cathedral. As we walked down those huge stone steps, I could not help but remember Psalm 122:1: "I rejoiced with those who said to me, 'Let us go to the house of the Lord.'"

After two weeks, I returned home to this relatively new community in southern Alberta to find everything seemed diminished in size and farther apart. The history of the settlers here, many who came from Britain and Scotland, barely spans one hundred and fifty years, and our country-side is so large compared to the fields and farms in England.

The next Sunday, I went to church in the tiny log church, which, although barely holding one hundred souls, is our local historical site. Built in 1869 with the cooperation, hard work, and donations of many of those first settlers, it stands in this community as a monument to their courage and faith. Many left a beautiful home and family to come here, where they established  this new country, bringing with them the traditions of family, government, and church that we still celebrate today. Our little church could fit in the front foyer of Westminster Abbey, but it holds for us the same beacon of faith represented by that amazing, awe-inspiring structure in London.

Today, I was reminded of this experience by the smell of the rain-soaked hayfields and these verses:

> When can I go and meet with God?
> While men say to me all day long,
> "Where is your God?"
> These things I remember when I pour out my soul:
> How I used to go with the multitude,
> Leading the procession to the house of God,
> With shouts of joy and thanksgiving among the
>   festive throng (Psalm 42:2-5).

Whiter Than Snow

April showers bring May flowers. Well, at least that's how the rhyme goes, but April this year, 2011, was somewhat colder than we would have liked, and so all the showers became the solid white variety. But after seven months of the solid white stuff and no Chinook to warm us up, people were becoming surly and even downright miserable. Normally lovely ladies have been unable to say a decent good morning when they came to our shop and older men only huffed as they stamped their feet and rubbed frostbitten fingers. The only ones who are truly happy are the young people with skis strapped to the top of their cars heading for the hills.

I have to admit I have been longing to be rid of the white stuff too and am sick of scraping frost from my windshield. All I want is to see a few blades of green grass! So when I looked out this morning, April 20, and saw a fresh fall of the sparkling white stuff covering the foot of old gray snow along the driveway, my first impulse was to scream, "NO! NO MORE! I CAN'T TAKE IT!" I complained and groused as I cleared the front walk and pushed the heavy white covering off the car. "Stop already! Surely there is warm air somewhere in the world!" I lamented as I tried to thaw my frozen fingers.

Then my grandchildren got up, and with the enthusiasm only children can generate, they ooh-ed and aah-ed over the new snow, planning their day around making snowmen and building forts. When the sun came out from behind the clouds, the true beauty of the fresh blanket was revealed as the yard turned into a magical place, sparkling with jewels as if God had sprinkled a million diamonds there. The brilliance of it hurt the eyes! My little grandson, who is a really deep thinker, said, "I know you don't want the snow, but this covered the dirty old bits, and now it's whiter than snow!" That set my heart to humming the old song, "Whiter than snow, yes, whiter than snow. Now wash me, and I shall be whiter than snow."

After I delivered the children to school, I looked for Bible references to snow. Psalm 147:16 says, "He spreads the snow like wool and scatters the frost like ashes." So we know that God sends the frost and snow. Further, Isaiah 55:10 tells us, "As the rain and the snow come down from heaven, and do not return to it without watering the earth and making it bud and flourish, so that it yields seed for the sower and bread for the hungry." We must trust that God in His wisdom knows what the earth needs and so will provide.

Still, the old song persisted in earworm fashion. I went on to read Psalm 51:7, where David asks to be washed with hyssop so he would be made whiter than snow. Considering the terrible sins David had committed, he had great confidence in God's grace to forgive and cleanse him. I was interested in the use of hyssop mentioned in this verse, so I looked for information about this plant. I found that it is abundant in the Middle East all the way down into Egypt, is known to have cleansing and purgative properties, and was the prescribed plant for both medicinal and ritual cleansing.

Finally, I found Isaiah 1:18, which is the basis for the song: 'Come, let us reason together,' says the Lord. 'Though your sins are like scarlet, they shall be white as the snow; though they are red as crimson, they shall be like wool.'

So I sit here, looking out my library window at the sparkling new blanket that covers the dirty, old brown stuff, and say a humble prayer of thanks for the reminder that Jesus came to be the cleansing hyssop for this sinful, old world and that His sacrifice is the cover that makes us appear whiter than snow before God the Father. Jesus is the cover and propitiation for our sins, without which we would never be allowed into the presence of God.

I looked up the old song written by William G. Fischer in 1876 now found in my copy of the North American Baptist Hymnal and went off singing.

Whiter Than Snow

Lord Jesus, I long to be perfectly whole, I want Thee forever to live in my soul; Break down every idol, cast out every foe;

Lord Jesus, look down from Thy throne in the skies, and help me to make a complete sacrifice; I give up myself, and whatever I know.

Lord Jesus, for this I most humbly entreat, I wait, blessed Lord, at Thy crucified feet; By faith, for my cleansing, I see Thy blood flow.

Lord Jesus, Thou see me, I patiently wait, come now, and within me a new heart create; To those who have sought Thee, Thou never said "NO."

Chorus: Now wash me, I shall be whiter than snow. Whiter than snow, yes whiter than snow; Now wash me, and I shall be whiter than snow.

Nothing to Fear but Fear

Have you ever watched a sports event, such as football or the Olympics, and become so totally absorbed in the game that you even forget to eat? In 2010, I watched the Olympics, and considering that I'm not much of a sports enthusiast, I didn't think that I would become so involved. However, I began watching a few events when I had time, and then to my surprise, I found myself completely mesmerized and in total awe of the athletes' skills. I cheered! I held my breath! And I cried with the competitors who did not succeed! I admit it; I became a flag-waving Canadian sports enthusiast that week.

Aside from the competitions, the segment that Rick Hansen, Man in Motion, did for TV, *The Difference Makers*, was also interesting. He came out, wheeling his chair between large pictures of people's faces and introduced us to specific athletes as well as the personal challenges that he or she had encountered while preparing to enter the Olympics. Then he introduced us to another person who was perhaps the competitor's friend, parent, sibling, or coach and recounted how that individual had made a significant difference in the athlete's life. In some cases, their actions had rescued that person from the pit of despair or addiction with friendship and love. In other cases, they came alongside with coaching and encouraging words that helped them onward and upward through injuries or emotional trials to eventual success. In all cases, the athletes said they would not have reached their dream of competing and winning a medal in the Olympics without the support of that particular individual.

As I read Philippians chapter three it was as if God had prepared it for this story. I could not help but hear these words form verse 13 and 14 reflected in what the athletes had said, "But this one thing I do: forgetting what is behind and straining toward what is ahead, I press on toward the goal (then we, who have Christian beliefs, can relate to the end of this verse as it defines our goal with these words) for which God has called me heavenward in Christ Jesus."

I was in awe of these athletes' courage as I watched them, particularly the skiers doing aerials and the slalom. When I

was younger, I stood at the top of a really challenging black diamond ski run and felt the fear and anxiety of attempting to make that run successfully to the bottom without falling or breaking something. So when I watched those athletes come out of the starting gate and twist and turn in flight down the hill, I wondered what makes them want to participate in this dangerous and challenging sport and how they overcame their fear.

One of the athletes said that it is not the course, the other athletes, or the competition rules that is the greatest hindrance to winning, but rather that fear is the greatest adversary. Franklin Delano Roosevelt said, "We have nothing to fear but fear its self!"

Fear weakens our resolve and causes us to become faint of heart. Perhaps it is the fear of failure or of what others will think or say that prevents the athlete, and even ourselves, from winning the medal or becoming successful in our careers, artistic endeavours or relationships. For this reason, many athletes have needed counselors, mentors, and coaches to come alongside for assistance. Many have consulted with older athletes who have competed in the past and are able to teach them the technical aspects of the sport and help them break through their insecurity.

Many athletes gain inspiration from someone close to them. For example, Alexandre Bilodeau attributes his tenacity and ability to persevere to the inspiration he receives from watching his older brother Frederick, who struggles with muscular dystrophy but doesn't let it defeat him. We could see that Fredrick is Alexandre's greatest fan and vise versa. These two brothers inspire and encourage each other to push through the pain and challenges that would defeat most individuals' spirit. Their wonderful example of brotherly love challenges us to share this same spirit with those around us.

It was interesting to note that only a handful of athletes began their competition with a prayer or the sign of the cross, and I heard only one, Cindy Klassen, the speed skater from Winnipeg, openly give the credit for her success to God.

During the ten days I watched the success and failures of the Olympic athletes, I encountered people in our community who were dealing with heartrending situations. I met people who were suffering because of job loss, those fighting cancer, a young woman struggling to overcome the scars of an abusive childhood, and another young woman who cried because her husband had rejected her after only one year of marriage. I talked to a gentleman who was suffering the scars of racial discrimination and another crying for a son caught in drug addiction.

These people were facing challenges as great as those faced by the Olympic athletes, and I felt overwhelmed by the stories they shared with me. So I turned to the Scripture lessons for that week and couldn't help but relate the events of the week to those lessons. After reading, I had to ask, "Was the lesson a coincidence?" I don't believe so, but allow me to share what I found so that you too will understand.

In every case, I heard the person express fear. Fear of the system, fear of the huge challenge they faced, fear of being alone, fear of the unknown, and even fear of death—just like those athletes had expressed. So when I offered my friendship, love, and encouragement to each person, I also included the promises of God that were the foundation for the meager comfort I offered.

I found reassurance in Isaiah 43:1-2, which is a promise from God to Jacob but is so relevant to us in the here and now:

> Fear not, for I have redeemed you; I have called you by name; you are mine. When you pass through waters I will be with you; and when you pass through the rivers, they will not sweep over you. You walk through fire, you will not be burned; the flames will not set you ablaze. For I am the Lord your God.

Another encouraging passage is found in the Psalms 46: 10 where David says, "The Lord is my light and my salvation, whom shall I fear? The Lord is the stronghold of my life, of whom shall I be afraid?" And in Proverbs 1:33, we find further encouragement in these words "Whoever listens to me will live in safety and be at ease without fear of harm." The Scriptures reassure us that God is with us when we face an uncertain future, rejection, and even the pain of death!

As I read God's Word, He allows me to live His grace in my everyday experiences. I just pray that God will give me the right message to help those who share their stories with me to overcome their fear in some way, as the mentors who helped the athletes as they prepared for their Olympic challenge.

I love the message I found in Luke 12:32:

> Do not be afraid, little flock, for your Father has been pleased to give you the kingdom. Sell your possessions and give to the poor. Provide purses for yourselves that will not wear out, a treasure in heaven that will not be exhausted, where no

thief comes to threaten or destroy. For where your
treasure is, there your heart will be also.

I have found that my treasure is in assisting another to
overcome their fear by reassuring them that God loves them
and will be with them in all situations.

A Christmas Story: The Birth of Baby J

The month of November had been cold and blustery, gray and depressing. Beginning with All Hallowed Eve on October 31, the bare trees were stark reminders that winter was just around the corner. Everyone was bundled up in winter parkas and scarves as they hurried home from their jobs in the gloomy light of early evening. The wind had been gusting to seventy-five kilometres per hour most of the day, raising dust and debris from the parking lot next door. It was a typical November evening gloomy and depressing. The green of summer was gone, and the streets were full of fallen leaves and garbage blowing before a heartless, cold wind.

Just as the lights were coming on for the evening, the wind gave a particularly strong blast, causing the building to shudder and the big glass door of the shop to open as if by an unseen hand. When I looked up, I saw a young native couple. She was holding her light jacket up over her head and face, trying to keep the dust out of her eyes. He had an arm around her shoulders, protecting and guiding her as they were pushed along by the gusty wind. They came straight across the parking lot toward the shop, and I could see they were in trouble before they came through the door. Their faces and hands were red and grimy from the cold and dirt carried by the ferocious wind. She was shivering as she stepped inside, and I saw that she was very pregnant. It was not the type of night that a person who was dressed in heavy clothing wanted to be outdoors for very long, and this young woman wore only a sweat suit and a light nylon jacket.

"Sorry to bother you, ma'am," the young man began. "I'm Joe Little Bear, and this is my wife, Marie. We came to the city a week ago lookin' for work, but I guess it's the wrong time of the year for construction. Anyway, we ran out of money, and we need help. My wife, well, she can't stay outside another night in her condition."

I groaned inwardly when I saw them coming toward our dry cleaning shop. We seem to be a magnet, with our bright lights and friendly front counter, for the homeless and wayward who roam the avenue looking for a kind face that might give them a dollar or two. I usually try to give them a voucher for food or coffee instead of cash that could be spent on the next bottle of alcohol or on drugs. But this case was different, so told I them to have a seat in the front office while I made a call to see if I could find some help for them. Joe expressed his thanks many times over and apologized profusely for the trouble as I looked up the phone number for the local church that had a program to house the homeless in their basement.

I reached Jean, the secretary, just in the nick of time. "I have my coat on to go home," she said, "so the front door will be locked. But the caretaker will be here, and they can come to the side door. I'll make sure he knows they are coming."

I told Joe and Marie where they could find a hot meal and a bed for the night, and that maybe in the morning someone there would be able to point them toward a more permanent solution to their problems.

About a week later, Jean phoned me back, "Hey, that was sure a nice young couple you sent over the other night. I think someone from the congregation needed a construction worker, so he has a job, and we got them into temporary housing until they can get a little money saved."

"I'm so glad to hear that! I was worried about her, in her condition. If they didn't get some help . . . well, who knows what could have happened. Thank goodness for the Inn from the Cold volunteers," I said.

"Say, that set me to thinking," Jean said hesitantly. "Would you be able to help us out? We have about thirty blankets that need to be washed every time we host an Inn, and I thought your big machines could make short work of washing and drying them."

I was taken by surprise and stammered a little, not knowing how to answer her.

Jean quickly gathered that I was not sure. "You think about it, and I'll send Dr. Bill to see you in a week or so. He can give you more information. If you can't, you can't . . . . but please think about it."

One week later, I committed to helping with washing the blankets for the homeless families that could not afford a damage deposit even though they might be working. I had always said it was a shame that so many went without in our rich province. At one time, I had been a poor single mother with two children, and although I worked hard, I often had only the next paycheck standing between the three of us and the street. I had often received help from family and friends during those years, so now that I was in a better position financially, it was time for me to pay it forward.

December came and with it a brilliant white snowfall to cover the gray of November. That along with the Christmas music on the radio lifted everyone's spirits. I had almost forgotten the young couple until Dr. Bill brought the bags and bags of blankets from the Inn three days before Christmas.

"Remember the young native couple you sent over? Well, he stopped in today to tell us that his wife was admitted to hospital this morning. He was on the way to see her and promised to let us know when the baby is born. I won't see you before Christmas 'cause I'm takin' the wife on a cruise. Surprise gift for her! Merry Christmas! I guess someone will come for the blankets and they will let you know the latest."

We always closed early on Christmas Eve, so I decided to take the blankets to the church before I went home to get ready for the midnight service. When I walked into the foyer of the church, there was the beautiful crèche, sitting among pine boughs on the table. As I came closer, my arms full of blankets, I saw sitting by the manger a picture of the young native couple with their new baby boy cuddled between them. A small sign leaning against the manger said, "Donations

gratefully accepted for baby J." I was pleased to see more than a few dollars had already been donated.

The Inn from the Cold program began in Saint Stephen's Anglican Church, Calgary, Alberta in 1997, and is run entirely by volunteers. Today it continues to serve the homeless from more than a hundred churches in Calgary, Alberta. The growth is largely due to the economic conditions of our community. In memory of Joe, Marie, and Baby J, I wish a Merry Christmas to each and everyone!

The following poem was written by myself as a tribute to the volunteers who work at the 'Inn' program and previously published in the Saint Stephen's Church December newsletter after the young couple mentioned in the previous story had come in my front door at the dry cleaners.

There But for the Grace of God

I travelled one day on the road of my life,
I'd had little pain and I'd had little strife.
Secure in the love of family and friend,
On God's Grace and His blessings, I had come to depend!

Then I met a wee child, all blue with the cold
And I listened a while to the story he told.
I sighed with some pity, as by me he passed.
"There but for God's Grace!" I quoted at last!

I met an old man, all dirty and grim
I wrinkled my nose at the awful smell of him.

I said, as I left him in his filth and his sin,
"But for God's Grace, I'd be like him."

A widow came by all dressed in her rags.
All earthly processions she kept in some bags.
Embarrassed, I stated, "I could not be like her
Thank God for his Grace!" as I stroked my warm fur.

I met a young man who could not seem to think.
His brain was befuddled by drugs and by drink.
I inquired, "Why are you living out here on the street?"
I thought with some pride, "Thanks to God's Grace,
my son's on his feet!"

I met a large family so pathetic and poor.
Although they were working, they slept on a floor.
"Why don't they save?" I wanted to know.
"The Grace of God's wisdom surely does show!"

Then at the end of the road, I saw my own self,
All haggard and old, put by, on the shelf,
Stinking and dirty with sin and in pain.
I cried out for God's Grace again and again!

Then in my distress, came the poor child to share
warmth with me.
And the old man, though dirty, spoke of salvation free.
The widow explained how to cope when alone.
And the young man's sweet smile made me feel right at home.
The large family came last with a share of their love.
Now I conclude, it was Grace from above,
That taught me to understand those lessons so old,
As I took each of these 'Inn' from the Cold!

—Linda Penton

The Littlest Angel

In a small village in Mexico, a potter named Pablo, who usually made ordinary clay pots and bowls of different colours and shapes to be used in kitchens, sat looking at the lump of clay he had set on his potter's wheel. Even though he knew everyone in the village and countryside appreciated them, he was bored making the same old things, day in day out. Being a potter was a good trade, and the sale of the bowls and pots paid for the house he and his family lived in and the food they ate, but it didn't satisfy his need to be a real artist. He felt a stirring in his heart and recognized it as a desire to be bold and do something different. But he knew that everyone trusted him to make his usual pots and bowls for their homes, so after a minute, he gave a big sigh and started to pedal, making the wheel spin round and round so he could begin another day's work.

Resigned to making an ordinary bowl, Pablo put his hands on the clay and began to shape it gently as it spun. But to his surprise, instead of the ordinary round pot that he was expecting, he saw a new and unusual figure emerging from the clay. He couldn't believe his eyes, because he thought he had not done anything different with his hands. The clay just seemed to take on a life of its own, and no matter what he did, the new shape grew.

At last, he slowed the wheel, and to his surprise, he saw the figure of a lovely lady with a long, flowing gown coming out of this ordinary lump of red clay. He finally stopped the wheel entirely and completed the lady with arms that he formed out of the bits that had fallen to the floor. Then he picked up a tiny, round ball and gently shaped it into a sweet-looking face. Last of all, he found two scraps that had fallen from the wheel that already were in the shape of perfect wings, so with just a little more work, he made them look like feathers and fastened them to her back with a piece of soft clay. He stood back and looked at her. To his delight, without even trying, Pablo had molded a beautiful angel.

This gave him a fantastic idea. He called to his wife, Maria, who was amazed. She knew her husband was a talented potter, but she had no idea he was so artistic. He was bubbling over with excitement when he told her his plan to make a new line of clay angels to sell in the marketplace. "Just for the market during the holiday season!" he pleaded with his wife. He was feeling the first twinges of real hope that made his heart beat fast for the first time in many years. She agreed, and so they quickly hauled in more clay, and Pablo began to work feverishly.

Soon, he had a whole row of angels of all sizes and shapes ready to go into the kiln, the hot oven that baked and hardened the clay. Some had halos, some were singing, some played musical instruments, and some were to be hung as if they were flying.

When the light grew dim near the end of the day, Pablo had only a small ball of clay left. Because they were poor, he was not in the habit of wasting anything, so he began to shape a very small angel. She was especially beautiful even though she was the smallest one of all. She had long, flowing sleeves and he had shaped her hands and arms perfectly as if she was holding something. But what would he put in her outstretched hands? Just then, a dove landed on the windowsill and cooed as if in answer to his question. Quickly, Pablo gathered up the last small bits of clay from the edge of the wheel, shaped them into a miniature replica of the dove, and gently placed it in her hands. The angel seemed to come to life right there on the board, and the dove seemed to lift its wings just a little higher when it was placed in the angel's hands. Shaking his head, Pablo said, "I've been working too long in this place. I'm beginning to imagine things. I need a break." He put all the angels into the kiln and went into the house for supper.

Meanwhile, far away in the country of Canada, a man named Dave and his wife, Eileen, were planning a holiday. They worked in a lovely gift shop in the city of Calgary called Ten Thousand Villages, and every year, they and other members of the Mennonite Church Central Committee travelled to faraway places to find beautiful handmade articles they could sell in their fair trade shops. Earlier this year, they had travelled to Pablo's village and were delighted to meet this talented artist and his wife in the marketplace. They had bought many of Pablo's lovely colored pots and bowls, which had sold like hotcakes. Customers were asking if they could get more, so they were going to visit Pablo again during their holiday in order to buy more of his wares.

When they arrived at the village, they could hardly believe their eyes. Pablo's stall in the marketplace was double its normal size, and there were so many customers they could hardly squeeze through the crowd. Instead of the gaily painted yellow, blue, and red pots they had expected, they found the shelves lined with angels of every shape and size which were painted white and pink and pale blue. The flying ones held streamers of stars or long French horns, and a choir held pages of music in their hands. The angels were so realistic that Dave and Eileen could almost hear them singing.

On the next shelf were musical angels holding harps, violins, and trumpets. On another shelf, some were sitting, some were kneeling, and some were standing tall with arms out stretched. All the angels had words like *Love*, *Faith*, *Believe*, and *Peace* painted on the banners they held or printed across the folds of their flowing skirts. Eileen clapped her hands in delight, and Dave immediately went to find Pablo to tell him they would buy as many as he could spare to ship back to the gift shop in Canada. That afternoon, after they had built the wooden crates and carefully packed the angels in straw for the long trip back to Calgary, Dave, Eileen, Pablo and Maria sat down to a fine traditional Mexican meal that Maria had made for them.

Back in Calgary about two months later, on a cold day in November, I came looking for a very special gift. I had become friends with the staff of Ten Thousand Villages while shopping at this marvelous store. We had discovered we had a similar family history, with grandparents of the Mennonite faith who had left the Ukraine many years before. This year, my mother, Julia, had broken her hip, so now, because she could no longer walk or look after herself, she lived in a senior citizens lodge about two blocks from the store.

As the year progressed, Julia became deeply depressed because she could no longer attend church, shop, or do any of the things she used to do. And living with so many other people in the home where she had to do as she was told instead of what she wanted was difficult. Mom had always been so independent and had kept a lovely home. She loved to celebrate the Christmas season by baking, cooking, and her own special brand of hospitality. Now in this place, the old lady from the room across the hall, who had forgotten her own name and didn't know what she was doing most days, invaded Mom's room, stealing the pictures of grandchildren and eating the treats that the family had brought for her.

That day in early November, I had stopped at the lodge to visit my mother on her way to work. I did not find her in her room, in the halls, or the sunroom. Finally, a kind nurse directed me to the chapel where I found mother with her head down on the altar, praying. When I gently asked her what she was praying for, she answered, "I'm asking Jesus to take me home."

"But, Mom, you know you can't go back home, because you can't walk. I thought we finished this discussion, and you agreed we wouldn't talk about it anymore!"

"I know that!" Mom snapped as if I was the one who was confused. "I'm not asking to go back to my house! I'm asking

Jesus to take me out of this place to be with Him! I don't belong here anymore, and I just want *some peace*!"

When I left the lodge, I knew I had to find some way to make the Christmas season special for my precious mother. I thought of buying her a warm sweater or a new dress, but knew that those things were not important to mother anymore. Julia didn't eat much, saying the food in the lodge tasted like sawdust. Suddenly, I had an idea. What if we rented the sunroom for an afternoon and everyone brought food and had a good, old family meal like we had shared at her house years ago?

As I drove by the Ten Thousand Villages Shop that day after the visit I decided to stop in to see the latest treasures on display and visit with friends in the hope of finding a little cheer. I wandered through the store, enjoying the beautiful displays of clay angels fresh from the Mexican potter, Pablo. Even though they symbolized the good cheer of the Christmas season, my heart remained heavy. At last, Dave and Eileen saw me and came to see if they could help me.

I told them about mother and how sad she was. "I'm just hoping to find something that will make her smile again." I finished the story with tears streaming.

"Come with me," Eileen said. She led me into the back of the store to her office, where she placed a small clay angel

gently into my hands. She was only seven or eight inches tall, molded in the Mexican tradition. Her long, flowing dress was painted white, which set off her ruddy, brown complexion and long, black hair. In her outstretched hands, she held a tiny white dove and across her skirt was painted the word *Peace*. Eileen explained that this was the smallest of all the angels they had brought from their trip to see Pablo, and that the dove had shaken loose during the long journey from Mexico. Eileen had re-glued it that very morning and sensed that the angel was unique, so she was determined to find a very special home for her. She told me that she felt the little angel's destiny was to bring good cheer to mother. I left the shop that day clutching the little *Peace* angel, feeling much better, determined to arrange a visit with the whole family for sometime in the first week of December when they could share some food, decorate mother's room, and present the little angel to her.

On the evening of December 5, 2002, I had stopped at the Safeway store at Glenmore Landing to pick up a few groceries for the meal we planned to prepare and take to the lodge the next day, when the family would meet to have their special time together. They had agreed upon a potluck dinner of Mother's favourite dishes and others were bringing decorations and gifts that would hopefully cheer her up.

While I was in the store, my cell phone rang. It was the nurse from the emergency ward at the Rocky View Hospital, informing me that mother had been admitted and was asking for her children. When I and my siblings arrived, the doctors told us that Mom had suffered a very serious heart attack and would probably not survive the night. So the family gathered around her bed side, and the four children each took turns holding their mother's hand saying their good-byes. When it was my turn she asked in a wee small voice, filled with the burden of her ninety years, if I could please say the Lord's Prayer with her and with that she finished her testimony to me with an example of how to finish well with grace and dignity.

Then in the small hours of the morning, as the flame of the prayer candle her grandson Axel had lit for her flickered out, God answered our sweet mother Julia's prayer. He gave her the peace she had asked for as He took her home to spend Christmas with Him in glory.

That was just before Christmas the first year we had moved to Millarville and we had just begun to attend Christ Church Anglican. When the ladies decorated the church for Christmas that year, I asked Reverend Pat if I could place the little Peace angel, which I had never had the opportunity to present to Mom, on the table near the Peace candle in memory of her. Here in this humble little log church, the little angel with her message of Peace, has found her home. I think Mom would like that!

The reading on that Sunday was taken from Luke chapter 2. verse 13 is very appropriate to remember the occasion "Suddenly, a great company of the heavenly host appeared with the angel, praising God and saying, 'Glory to God in the highest, and on earth peace to men on whom his favour rests'" (Luke 2:13).

A Golden Jubilee

Since 1962, the women of Christ Church, Millarville have decorated the historic Anglican Church and the cemetery next to it with flowers from their gardens and the surrounding fields on the third Saturday of July. They were first inspired to hold a Flower Festival by Mrs. J. R. King, who had attended a similar event in England that year. The ladies decided this would be a fine way to celebrate the historical significance of the church as well as to raise funds for the maintenance of the church and grounds. They have continued to host a tea in conjunction with the festival for the last forty-nine years.

In those first years, the women made fancy sandwiches and cookies that they served for both days, Saturday and Sunday, along with gallons of tea, coffee, and cold drinks to all who came. A well-meaning and well-connected lady from the area once had public notices about the event published in the *Calgary Herald* and broadcasted on CBC Radio. To the horror of the women serving, the people came by the car and bus loads, exhausting the supply of food the ladies had prepared and that of the local stores in the surrounding community, not to mention the women's energy. Although they now laugh about that event and refer to that year as *a bit of a gong show*, they still shudder if anyone suggests we run an ad in the paper or put the announcement on the radio.

Over the years, the food has changed. Today, we serve a traditional high tea only on Saturday with scones, whipped cream, and fresh strawberry conserve as fare. The year 2012 will mark the fiftieth anniversary of this festival with its now famous Strawberry Tea which will be served once again at Church House on July 21st, 2012. The women charge a small fee of six dollars for the refreshments, which, considering the amount of time and effort that goes into the preparations, is very reasonable. This is a refreshing stop for our local neighbors as well as passing travelers and a chance to visit and learn a bit about the history of the area. The funds raised will again be used for the maintenance of this historical log church and the beautiful grounds that surround it.

The event has grown in notoriety by word of mouth, simply because it is old-fashioned and so fitting for commemorating the history of this 116 year old log church and the people who built it. People come from towns as far as two or three hundred miles away, with many returning year after year for tea, and are invited to worship with us on Sunday. That special service is graced with as many as fifty bouquets all contributed by parishioners or by the children of those who once worked and worshipped here. The cemetery is a testament to the settlers of the area and is likewise decorated to honour past members.

This weekend requires much cooperation and hard work of the women in this congregation assisted by the Millarville Horticultural Society. Although many are not young any more, they still contribute their time and talents without reserve or complaint. In fact, we chat and tease each other good-naturedly as we prepare dishes of whipped cream and strawberry jam to go with the scones and tea. Then we all pitch in to clean up or wash dishes after the event. The ladies who serve, dressed in their colourful dresses and frilly, white aprons, are like butterflies in a field of flowers as they work together to serve the hundreds of people who come to support this special occasion.

In honour of the Golden Jubilee of the Flower Festival and all who have contributed to its success, I have written the following poem.

Walking with God Among the Flowers

I awoke one morn and left my room,
To walk out in the woods.
To say a prayer and offer thanks,
For all my worldly goods.

I left the path and wandered far
Beneath the aspen trees.
My words, I found, were idle chatter
When compared to the buzz of honeybees.

The birds and flowers offered up their praise,
More eloquent than words.
My morning prayers were but a sham,
In contrast with the song of birds.

The grasses nodded humble heads
At the urging of the breeze.
And the willows wept their penitence,
While deer bent humbly on their knees.

In soaring praise, the birds took flight
Across a cloudless sky.

And flowers lifted radiant blooms,
To worship God on high.

Roses blushed in quick response
To kisses from the sun.
Their incense rises up to God
From morn until the day is done.

The clover blossoms, white and pink,
Add sweetness to the air.
Giving God's aromatherapy,
To soothe our every care.

The coneflowers lift their purple heads
In early morning praise.
And black-eyed Susan add their smiles
To this, gentlest of days.

Buttercups and violets hide
Low among the grass.
Inspiration they provide
To those of us who pass.

God clothed the lilies of the field
In orange and purest gold.
"Teach us, dear Lord, to worry less
And trust your promises of old."

Down by the stream, Jack-in-the-pulpit
Will preach his best today.
And sphagnum moss provides a bench
Where I can kneel to pray.

The Indian plume, bright orange and red,
Adorn the roads and trails.

And goldenrod is God's own treasure
Among the new-formed bales.

Delphinium and shooting stars
In purple riot bloom.
Side by side a bright contrast
To this world of pain and gloom.

Dogwood, with their blood-red stems,
Wave their sweet, white flowers.
Reminding us of Christ's shed blood
And of His saving powers.

Waving in the morning breeze,
Were plants of every kind.
Growing there together,
Every colour you could find.

Some plants were tall and lanky,
With their blossoms way up high,
And some were low and creeping,
With subtle colour for the eye.

Some were large with showy leaves
And great big, shining faces.
And some had tiny little flowers,
Which grew in rocky places.

So like the human family,
This field of flowers grows.
Each one unique and special,
Each one, God surely knows.

But better still, to see the field
With flowers all combined.

In harmony, they work so well,
God's nature to define.

What shall I be? What shall I do?
So often I have ranted.
I've learned today out in that field,
To bloom, just where I'm planted.

The End

I end this book with these words written by Paul to the Corinthians and his words are my humble submission to you the reader:

> When I came to you, brothers, I did not come with eloquence or superior wisdom as I proclaimed to you my testimony about God. For I resolved to know nothing while I was with you except Jesus Christ and Him crucified. I came to you in weakness and fear and with much trembling. My message and my testimony were not with wise and persuasive words, but with a demonstration of the Spirit's power, so that your faith might not rest on men's wisdom, but on God's power and wisdom. I Corinthians 2: 1-5
>
> Amen, So let it be.

CPSIA information can be obtained at www.ICGtesting.com
Printed in the USA
LVOW080231171012

303122LV00003B/8/P